THE HISTORY OF THE U.S. MARSHALS

THE HISTORY OF THE
U.S. MARSHALS

THE PROUD STORY OF AMERICA'S LEGENDARY LAWMEN

by Robin Langley Sommer

COURAGE
BOOKS

Picture Credits

All pictures courtesy of The Bettmann Archive, except the following:

Brompton Picture Library: 68-69; 70 top; 71 both
Chicago Historical Society: 90-91 top
The Detroit News, photo by Pete Brooks: 87
Courtesy The Historic New Orleans Collection; 36-37 top
Collection IBM Corporation, Armonk, New York: 26-27
Independence National Historic Park Collection: 10 left
The Kansas State Historical Society: 23-24 bottom
Stephen Laferney: 124-125 top
The Library of Congress: 13; 15; 16 bottom left; 20; 22; 33; 34 top; 38 top left; 82-83
Los Angeles Times-Bernie Boston: 116
Miami Herald, photo by David Walters: 121 top
National Archives: 32, 79
National Archives of Canada: 28 top
The New-York Historical Society: 18 bottom
The Oregonian, photo by Dana Olsen: 112 top
Reese Library, Augusta College: 12 top
Raymond Sherrard: 6 bottom left, top right; 37 right; 40 top; 48-49 all; 55 top left; 56-57 top; 66 bottom; 72 top; 76 bottom left; 78 top and center; 81; 90; 93 top and bottom left; 95 right; 97 both; 106 right; 107 all four; 119; 125 bottom left
Reuters: 121 bottom; 124 bottom
Sygma: J. L. Atlan: 6-7 bottom center; 108 bottom; 110-111; 112-113 bottom; 114; William Berry: 122 left; P. F. Gero: 108-109 top; Sygma: 7 top
UPI/Bettmann: 84; 86 top; 86-87 bottom; 88; 89 both; 98-99 all; 100; 101; 102-103 both; 104-105; 106 left; 115; 117 both; 118; 120; 122-123 bottom; 123 top; 125 bottom right
U.S.M.S. Photo Collection: 77; 93 right; 113 top; 126
Western History Collections, University of Oklahoma Library: 50-51; 52; 55 top right, bottom left, bottom right; 74 both; 76-77 top; 76 bottom right

Acknowledgments

The author and publisher would like to thank Adrian Hodgkins who designed the book, Florence Norton, the indexer, Elizabeth Montgomery the picture researcher, as well as Raymond Sherrard and George Stumpf, whose book *Badges of The United States Marshals*, proved invaluable, and Dave Turk and Jo Simpson of the U.S. Marshals Service.

CONTENTS

Introduction

When people hear the term "U.S. marshal" they often think first of frontier days and a lone man with a badge riding into a brawling cattle town to enforce the law. Others may recall the marshals' presence on Southern campuses and city streets of the 1960s in support of the civil rights movement. Viewers of the nightly news are familiar with the sight of U.S. deputy marshals escorting hooded figures from the Witness Protection Program into court, arresting terrorists and fugitives, and working with federal drug-enforcement officers to stop the traffic in illegal drugs. But few people are aware that U.S. marshals and their deputies are now in their third century of federal law enforcement. In 1989, the U.S. marshals celebrated their bicentennial as the nation's oldest and most authoritative law-enforcement officers.

The story of the U.S. marshals starts in 1789, when the new federal government established its judiciary system. The marshals and their deputies were commissioned to support and protect the federal courts in each judicial district. Thus, they became a vital link between the executive and judicial branches of the government. Today the U.S. Marshals Service has grown to include more than 3,000 deputy marshals and administrative personnel, operating from 427 offices in all 94 judicial districts nationwide and in the U.S. territories abroad.

ABOVE: *The first standardized marshals' badge: 1941.*

LEFT: *A specially produced marshal's badge in sterling silver featuring the U.S. shield as central motif.*

ABOVE: *Popular Stanley E. Morris served as director of the Marshals Service between 1983 and 1989.*

BELOW: *An SOG deputy takes aim. The Special Operations Group, formed in 1971, is trained for high-threat emergency situations.*

The marshals have been involved in every chapter of American history, from the Whiskey Rebellion of 1794 to the fight against illegal drugs in this morning's headlines. In the process they have often had to uphold unpopular federal laws like the Sedition Act of 1798 and the fugitive slave laws included in the Constitution to induce the Southern states to join the union. During the War of 1812 they registered and kept track of all British citizens living in the United States, arresting those who violated their agreements not to work against the government. Much of it was thankless, ill-paid work that set the U.S. marshal of each district and his deputies at odds with the local community.

Before and during the Civil War, the marshals were afflicted by the same polarization that beset the entire nation. On the one hand, they enforced the provisions of the despised Fugitive Slave Law in the North, often at the risk of their lives; on the other, they pursued slave ships in Southern waters to enforce the early nineteenth-century statute that made the African slave trade illegal.

Marshals in Confederate states resigned their commissions to President Abraham Lincoln in 1861, while those in Northern states pursued spies and traitors to the Union. The war's end brought the dangerous responsibility of enforcing the Civil Rights Act of 1866. In the South, this meant protecting black freedmen and their families from their former owners, and throughout the period of Radical Reconstruction, the U.S. marshals were in violent conflict with the Ku Klux Klan and other white-supremacist secret societies.

As the nation's frontier moved west, the marshals became the only federal lawmen in the unorganized territories that were on the road to statehood. The latter half of the nineteenth century saw them "on the scout" in Indian Territory, pursuing outlaws and vigilantes of every stripe, and policing the long Mexican border against raiders from both sides of the Rio Grande. This was the era of Billy the Kid and Deputy Marshal Pat Garrett, of the James gang and their train and stagecoach hold-ups, of the Clantons and their famous shoot-out with Wyatt Earp and his brothers at Tombstone's O.K. Corral.

As the nation struggled into the twentieth century, the marshals worked against widespread and violent strikes, registered enemy aliens during World War I, and sought to enforce the un-enforceable Volstead Act during the years of Prohibition. As other federal agencies, such as the Federal Bureau of Investigation, rose to prominence, the marshals found their role decreasing: they were generalists in an age of specialization. But during the civil rights confrontations of the 1960s, they performed so well that they won nearly universal admiration, and since then their duties and authority have increased dramatically. The story of the U.S. marshals spans some 200 years. Many chapters have yet to be written.

Lawmen for a New Nation

The first Congress of the United States created the offices of U.S. marshal and deputy marshal in the Judiciary Act of 1789, which established the federal judicial system. As a result, the marshals' history is inseparable from that of the federal courts, which they were authorized to support and protect. President George Washington appointed the first U.S. marshals to the district and circuit courts established by the new nation. These men were broadly empowered to carry out all lawful orders issued by judges, Congress, or the president. But they were also limited to four-year renewable terms and could be replaced at the president's pleasure.

During most of their history, the marshals hired their own deputies from within their judicial districts, usually seeking men (and later, women) who had close ties and credibility with the local community. This was especially important in the early days of our national life, when Federalist and Anti-Federalist factions faced off for their fierce struggle over the definition of federal authority. The U.S. marshals represented the newly created (and not fully fledged) central government within their jurisdictions, and hostility toward unpopular federal laws was often first directed at them.

Frederick S. Calhoun, official historian of the U.S. Marshals Service, summarized the marshals' original mandate in *The Lawmen*, published by the Smithsonian Institution Press in 1989:

> The primary function of the marshals was to support the federal courts. They served the subpoenas, summonses, writs, warrants, and other process issued by the courts; made all the arrests; and handled all the prisoners. They also disbursed the money, paying the fees and expenses of the court clerks, U.S. attorneys, jurors, and witnesses. They rented the courtrooms and jail space and hired the bailiffs, criers, and janitors.

In addition, the marshals were called upon to perform various tasks for the federal government by default, because there was no other administrative system in place throughout the states. For example, they took the national census every decade for 80 years, from 1790 to 1870. They also distributed presidential proclamations, collected

ABOVE: *Presidential appointment of U.S. marshals began with George Washington in 1789.*

RIGHT: Harper's Weekly *published this sketch of U.S. marshals taking the census in 1870.*

BELOW: *Simply getting to court was a challenge for early judges, marshals, and lawyers.*

statistics on commerce and industry, registered enemy aliens during wartime, exchanged spies and prisoners of war with foreign countries – in short, they functioned as the government's civilian police power. And for more than a century they were the only such power. Even today, with more than 50 specialized federal law-enforcement agencies in operation, the marshals have the broadest jurisdiction and authority. In fact, their role within the Justice Department is now larger and more diversified than ever before.

But in the nation's early years the position of U.S. marshal had many burdensome aspects – for one, there was no salary. Compensation was by various fees for services rendered, and these had to be collected from the government through a lengthy and laborious process that was not always successful. Moreover, each marshal also had to post a $20,000 bond to protect the government from any attempt by the marshal to cheat on the fees or to appropriate the funds he handled for the courts. There was no training for the job, and there was no job security. Unlike the U.S. attorneys with whom they worked, the marshals could be fired at any time, and renewal of their four-year terms required the concurrence of the Senate.

LEFT: *Nathaniel Ramsay, a Revolutionary War hero painted by Rembrandt Peale about 1794, was the first U.S. marshal for Maryland.*

RIGHT: *Secretary of the Treasury Alexander Hamilton joined the militia to enforce his tax policies during the Whisky Rebellion.*

ABOVE: *Revolutionary War general Henry Dearborn served as the first marshal for the District of Maine.*

RIGHT: *Illegal distillers in western Pennsylvania are warned that federal officers are nearby.*

For 60 years, until the 1850s, the marshals were loosely supervised by the secretary of state and had a high degree of autonomy within their districts. But they had to walk a delicate line between their official duties and their relationships within the community, especially when it came to enforcing an unpopular law such as the 1791 excise tax on whisky, which became an early test of the federal government's power.

Secretary of the Treasury Alexander Hamilton had proposed the tax on whisky to meet the new government's pressing need for revenue. The measure led to immediate and widespread objection, and especially in the four counties of western Pennsylvania. The settlers of Pennsylvania's Monongahela Valley, primarily Scotch-Irish in origin, counted on whisky for most of their income. Their wheat and grain crops were readily converted into cash with the help of homemade stills, and cash was a scarce commodity on what was

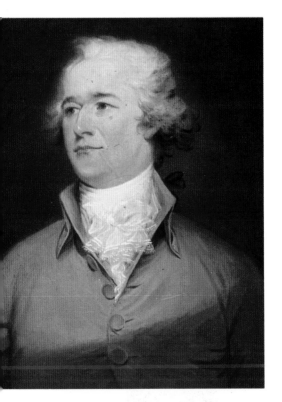

then the nation's outermost frontier. The idea of intrusive tax collectors invading the backwoods to mark their stills and demand money far in advance of their whisky sales was anathema. At a convention held in Pittsburgh in 1792 it was decided to resist the tax by every means. Indeed, individual attacks had already been made on several collectors and inspectors: the year before, Robert Johnson, the collector for Washington and Allegheny Counties, had been attacked by 16 men who tarred and feathered him and stole his horse – the first of many such incidents.

At the end of May 1794 violent opposition to the tax and outright refusal to pay it led the federal district court in Philadelphia, then the nation's capital, to issue summonses to 75 western-Pennsylvania distillers. U.S. Marshal David Lenox decided to ride across the state to serve the summonses himself, rather than sending a deputy. He was reasonably well received – until he got to Allegheny County.

There, accompanied by General John Neville, inspector of revenue for western Pennsylvania, Marshal Lenox attempted to serve a summons on a farmer named William Miller, who refused it. The officers were then fired upon by a mob of 30 to 40 men and left

the farm. The next morning, an armed mob appeared at Neville's home and a pitched battle ensued, in which five of the Whisky Rebels were killed. Shortly afterward, both Neville and Marshal Lenox were taken prisoner by some 500 rebels, from whom they barely escaped with their lives.

After Marshal Lenox made his report to Hamilton in early August, the government made plans to send combined state militias into western Pennsylvania under the command of Revolutionary War general "Lighthorse Harry" Lee of Virginia. Meanwhile, Attorney General William Bradford was sent into the embattled region to negotiate a peaceful settlement, if possible. By September 24 hundreds of the Whisky Rebels had signed an oath of allegiance to the government, but many remained recalcitrant, so the militiamen were ordered to Pittsburgh. Marshal Lenox rode with the militia to Pittsburgh, accompanied by U.S. Attorney William Rawle and Judge Richard Peters.

By November 13, almost 18 suspects had been arrested, but as there was no further organized resistance to the federal government, the few rebels who were convicted of treason were eventually pardoned. Marshal Lenox was instrumental in securing a presidential pardon for one Benjamin Parkinson, who had protected him from a group of drunken rebels during his dangerous foray into western Pennsylvania. Although the excise tax on whisky would

LEFT: *U.S. Marshal Robert Forsyth was shot and killed while serving court papers for the District of Georgia in 1794.*

RIGHT: *General Henry Lee, nicknamed "Lighthorse Harry," led combined state militias against the Whisky Rebels in western Pennsylvania.*

BELOW: *Government officials were tarred and feathered by insurrectionists during the Whisky Rebellion, which tested the power of the newly created federal government.*

continue to be widely resented until its repeal in 1809, the Whisky Rebellion had been effectively quelled by the new federal government.

The first of more than 400 marshals to be killed while carrying out their duties was Robert Forsyth, the first marshal for the District of Georgia. His murder occurred in 1794, in the course of his serving court papers on two brothers, William and Beverly Allen, during a civil suit. Accompanied by two deputies, Marshal Forsyth entered the house of an Augusta matron named Dixon and asked to speak privately to the Allens. For reasons unknown, the brothers refused to come outside with him and bolted upstairs, locking themselves in an empty room. When Forsyth followed them with his deputies, William Allen shot through the door and killed him. The shocked deputies arrested the brothers, but they later escaped from custody.

FIFTH CONGRESS OF THE UNITED STATES:

At the Second Session.

Begun and held at the city of *Philadelphia*, in the state of PENNSYLVANIA, on *Monday*, the thirteenth of *November*, one thousand seven hundred and ninety-seven.

An ACT in addition to the act, entitled 'An Act for the punishment of certain crimes aga the United States.'

BE it enacted by the Senate and House of Representatives of the United States of America, in Congress assembled. That if persons shall unlawfully combine or conspire together, with intent to oppose any measure or measures of the government of the United States, which are or be directed by proper authority, or to impede the operation of any law of the United States, or to intimidate or prevent any person, holding a place or office under the government of the United States, from undertaking, performing or executing his trust or duty; and if any person or persons, with intent aforesaid, shall, counsel, advise or attempt to procure any insurrection, riot, unlawful assembly, or combination, whether such conspiracy, threatening, advice, or attempt shall have the proposed effect or not, he or they shall be deemed guilty of a high misdemeanor, and on conviction, before any court of the United States having jurisdiction thereof, shall be punished by a fine not exceeding five thousand dollars, and by imprisonment during a term not less than months nor exceeding five years; and further, at the discretion of the court may be holden to find sureties for his good behaviour in such sum, and for such tim the said court may direct.

Sect. 2. And be it further enacted, That if any person shall write, print, utter or publish, or shall cause or procure to be written, printed, u or published, or shall knowingly and willingly assist or aid in writing, printing, uttering or publishing any false, scandalous and malicious writing or writ against the government of the United States, or either House of the Congress of the United States, or the President of the United States, with intent to de the said government, or either House of the said Congress, or the said President, or to bring them, or either of them, into contempt or disrepute; or to excite agains or either or any of them, the hatred of the good people of the United States; or to stir up sedition within the United States; or to excite any unlawful combinatio therein, for opposing or resisting any law of the United States, or any act of the President of the United States, done in pursuance of any such law, or of the p in him vested by the Constitution of the United States; or to resist, oppose, or defeat any such law or act; or to aid, encourage or abet any hostile designs of any nation against the United States, their people or government, then such person, being thereof convicted before any Court of the United States, having jurisdiction t shall be punished by a fine not exceeding two thousand dollars, and by imprisonment not exceeding two years.

Sect. 3. And be it further enacted and declared, That if any person shall be prosecuted under this act, for the writing or publishing a libel aforesaid, it shall be lawful for the defendant, upon the trial of the cause, to give in evidence in his defence, the truth of the matter contained in the publication charged as a libel. And the jury who shall try the cause, shall have a right to determine the law and the fact, under the direction of the Court, other cases.

Sect. 4. And be it further enacted, That this act shall continue and be in force until the third day of March, one thousand eight hund and one, and no longer:- Provided, that the expiration of the act shall not prevent or defeat a prosecution and punishment of any offence against t law, during the time it shall be in force.

Jonathan Dayton Speaker of the House of Representatives.

Theodore Sedgwick President of the Senate, pro tempore.

Approved July 14. 1798

John Adams
President of the United States

I certify that this Act did originat the Senate.

Attest

Sam A. Otis Se

LEFT: The text of the Sedition Act of 1798, which granted broad powers to arrest anyone accused of criticizing U.S. government policies or officers.

BELOW: A political cartoon of 1798 shows Republican congressman Matthew Lyon (center) attacking an opponent. Lyon was convicted of sedition for his criticism of Federalist policies.

In 1798 the marshals became involved in the enforcement of the new Alien and Sedition Acts, a malignant by-product of the growing animosity between the Republicans and the Federalists. The Sedition Act, in particular, posed a grave threat to freedoms granted by the Constitution. The precipitating cause was Republican support for the ideals of the French Revolution and for the revolutionary government that had overthrown the monarchy. The Federalists, led by President John Adams, were hostile to the new French government both because of its bloodthirsty excesses and its persistent interference with U.S. trading ships. The Federalists considered Republican criticism of their attitude toward France treasonous and passed three repressive measures to suppress it. The Alien Acts of June/July 1798 allowed the president to order deportation of any foreign national he identified as dangerous to the public safety, and, in wartime, to imprison such aliens as he judged loyal to the enemy. The Sedition Act of July 14 was even more dangerous in its implications for freedom of speech and the press, for it permitted the arrest of anyone who engaged in "false, scandalous, and malicious writing" about government policies or officers of the government, from the president on down.

Zealous Federalists such as Secretary of State Timothy Pickering scanned the Republican newspapers for "seditious" sentiments, and the U.S. marshals were charged with making the requisite arrests. Twenty-five Republican publishers, editors, and printers were arrested while the act was in force. One of them was publisher Ann Greenleaf, who lost her newspaper, the *Argus*, as a result, although she was never brought to trial. Her printer, David Frothingham, was both tried and convicted of libel against Alexander Hamilton – who was not even an officer of the government at the time when the action was brought.

During the 30-month period when the act was in force, ten people went to prison for their criticisms of Federalist policies and leaders, but one, the outspoken Matthew Lyon, a Republican Congressman from Vermont, proved to be a Tartar. He was convicted of sedition in October 1798 in the midst of his campaign for re-election to Congress. Sentenced to four months in prison and a $1,000 fine, Lyon was taken into custody by Marshal Jabez G. Fitch of the district of Vermont, whose Federalist sympathies were well

LEFT: *During Thomas Jefferson's second term as president, the unpopular Embargo Act of 1807 had to be enforced by U.S. marshals in ports where resistance occurred.*

ABOVE: *The struggle between Great Britain's Royal Navy and Napoleon's French fleet had an extremely adverse effect on U.S. shipping during the early 1800s.*

known. Fitch made Lyons' confinement as unpleasant as possible and even refused, for a time, to supply the Congressman with pen and ink for his campaign correspondence unless he submitted his letters for censorship. Fitch finally thought better of this matter, and Lyon was re-elected by a substantial majority. He had become a hero to the embattled Republicans and received both financial and moral support from such prominent party members as James Madison and Thomas Jefferson. When Jefferson became president two years later, Marshal Fitch lost his job, and so did 17 other marshals who had expressed Federalist sympathies.

As Frederick Calhoun points out in *The Lawmen*, "Quite simply, the office of marshal was a patronage job, subject to all the abuses of such a system." This political aspect of the position also made it difficult for the marshals to grow in experience and professionalism as a body. When a U.S. marshal was fired, his deputies generally went with him, and his successor had to start from scratch.

Throughout the first decade of the 1800s Great Britain and Napoleonic France steadily escalated their war on one another's international trade, and U.S. maritime commerce suffered accordingly. The unpopular Embargo Act of 1807, prohibiting all foreign trade, was the ineffectual response of Thomas Jefferson and his Congress. Customs collectors at every American port were responsible for enforcing this almost-unenforceable measure, with the assistance of the marshals when active resistance occurred. This was a real problem in the Northeast, where New England shipping had suffered greatly.

By 1809, when James Madison succeeded Jefferson, disputes between the U.S. and Great Britain over America's maritime trading rights had become acute, and incidents of Royal Navy ships intercepting U.S. merchentmen were multiplying. Finally, in June 1812, Congress declared war on the British. But if the U.S. hoped that the fact that Britain was simultaneously at war with France would help the U.S. cause, it was to be disappointed: the world's most powerful nation was quite able, if unwilling, to take on its erstwhile American colonies at the same time. The U.S. government soon had even more cause to regret its decision, for apart from the might of the British Navy and Army, there was major domestic opposition to the war.

It soon proved difficult to fill the ranks of some of the state militias. And there were thousands of British nationals with

ABOVE: *British soldiers and sailors burn the new U.S. Capitol in Washington, D.C., during the War of 1812.*

LEFT: *A British engraving shows the capture of the city of Washington on August 24, 1814. Almost 12,000 British aliens living in the United States were registered and controlled by the marshals during the war against Great Britain.*

American interests living in the country, a situation which posed a considerable threat of espionage and sabotage. Prisoners of war had to be maintained in custody after every engagement. In all these matters, the government turned to the marshals for help.

Enforcing the provisions of the Alien Act of 1798 was the marshals' biggest single job during the War of 1812 (which lasted until early 1815, if one includes the Battle of New Orleans on January 8, fought and won before news of the peace was received in the field). New deputies had to be appointed in every district to keep watch on British citizens residing in the United States. The British residents had to report to the deputies each month, and they compiled long lists of these registrants and their movements for the State Department. A total of 11,554 British aliens was reported and "controlled," during the war, which meant that the marshals also had to provide them with licenses and passports to travel at need. The British who lived near the coast had to be relocated farther inland, beginning early in 1813 when engagements were first fought on American soil. They were on their honor to stay at the interim locations, but these promises were not always kept, as the aliens were not confined or guarded.

In the summer of 1813, for example, Marshal John Smith of Pennsylvania arrested British citizen Charles Lockington of Philadelphia, who had violated his agreement to remain in Reading. Apparently, Lockington had returned home to provide military intelligence to British forces near Philadelphia. He was confined in a local prison for six months, until he took an oath to return to Reading for the duration. Similar cases of espionage were handled by U.S. marshals in Maine, Massachusetts, New York, Rhode Island, and Connecticut, where British citizens living on the coast were ordered inland to Tolland.

British prisoners of war presented a daunting problem in both maintenance and logistics. Four U.S. ports and two British stations, Halifax and Jamaica, were designated as sites for the exchange of prisoners by ship. The marshals at Salem, Massachusetts; Newport, Rhode Island; Wilmington, Delaware; and Charleston, South Carolina, fed and housed British prisoners until they could be exchanged, with all the paperwork attendant upon the process. For this work the marshals were – subsequently – paid the princely sum of seventy-five cents per prisoner handled.

During the two and a half years of the war, the United States had won only a few significant battles and had seen its new Capitol and White House in Washington, D.C., burned, before a British expedition to Chesapeake Bay was stopped at Baltimore. But throughout the conflict, officially ended by the Treaty of Ghent in December 1814, the marshals and their deputies had acquitted themselves well in their demanding roles as local executive officers who could be relied upon in an emergency.

The Slave Trade, Counterfeiters, and Adventurers Abroad

When the Constitution was drafted, representatives from the North and those from the South had reached an uneasy compromise on what was to prove the most divisive issue in U.S. history: slavery. The agricultural South was unanimous and adamant in its support of the institution, while the North distrusted it but gave it grudging

ABOVE: *U.S. marshals enforce the unpopular fugitive slave laws by arresting an escaped slave for return to the South.*

acceptance, primarily to induce the South to accept union. In the three sections of the Constitution that related to slavery, the divided mind of the nation could clearly be seen. First, three-fourths of the slaves in each state were counted to determine Southern membership in the House of Representatives. Second, the African slave trade was to continue for another 20 years before any law could be passed against it. Third, each state was to be responsible for returning fugitive slaves (called "fugitives from labor") to their legal owners.

When the 20-year limit on banning the African slave trade ran out in 1808, Jefferson suggested that the trade should be outlawed, and Congress concurred. In 1819 an even stronger measure defined the trade as piracy – a capital crime. Meanwhile, the fugitive slave laws applied equally in the North, where abolitionist sentiment was growing, and in the South, where property and regional rights were paramount. This conflict was mirrored in the anomalous situation of the U.S. marshals. Those in the North had to capture fugitive slaves and return them, often against violent opposition, while Southern marshals tried to interdict the slave trade that a vast majority of the citizens in their region supported.

The slavery issue became ever more envenomed throughout the first half of the nineteenth century, as Congress struggled to maintain some balance between free and slave states while the frontier moved steadily west. As with the slavery sections of the Constitution, few of the compromises reached were satisfactory to either faction.

Despite the rigorous penalty attached to the African slave trade in the 1819 statute, the government did little to enforce the measure during the succeeding decades, partly because of Southern opposition and partly because it had no follow-up plan. In 1820, for example, the revenue cutter *Dallas* caught a slave ship with 258 Africans aboard and delivered them to Marshal William Morel in Savannah after the traders were indicted. The grueling voyage had left many Africans sick or dying, but Morel had no facilities adequate for their care and housing. A plan to return such Africans to their native continent had gotten as far as a Congressional appropriation of $100,000 for the president's discretionary use in such cases, but it was hedged with so many restrictions that few of those rescued from the slave trade ever reached the coastal colony of Liberia that was finally established for that purpose. In this instance, Marshal Morel was finally reduced to the expedient of consigning the captured Africans to various plantations in the vicinity where he could only hope they would be well treated. Other marshals encountered similar problems in the rare cases when slave ships were captured by the small U.S. Navy.

Three ships were caught in Southern waters and one off Massachusetts in 1820, but the number of arrests for piracy was

LEFT: *Africans captured by the slave ship* Wildfire *are brought into a Florida port in defiance of the law against the slave trade.*

paltry compared to that of the slave ships that reached their destinations. And once they did, there was no law preventing the sale of slaves within the United States, or between the United States and other nations of the Western Hemisphere. Many plantation owners traveled to Cuba to buy Africans who had been transported there, then shipped them into the South. By 1850, however, Northern opposition to slavery was becoming more organized and vociferous, especially after the passage that year of the Fugitive Slave Law. Its provisions were harsher and more specific than those embodied in the Constitution, and Northern marshals faced considerable risk when they apprehended escaped slaves for return to the South, or arrested those who had helped them.

Municipal and state authorities often refused to cooperate in detaining a recaptured slave, as in the case of Frederick Jenkins, called Shadrach, who was arrested in Boston in 1851 by Deputy Marshal Patrick Riley of Massachusetts. The Bay State had passed a law prohibiting the rental of jail space for holding fugitive slaves, and the Boston Navy Yard refused Riley's request for a place to house his prisoner. Finally, with the help of two deputies as guards,

LEFT: *Pro- and anti-slavery factions face off in a political cartoon captioned "Practical Illustration of the Fugitive Slave Law."*

BELOW: *Free Staters in Kansas Territory, with headquarters in Lawrence, opposed enforcement of the fugitive slave laws by district deputy marshals.*

Riley imprisoned Jenkins in the courthouse, where two rooms were rented by the marshals to hold federal court. The mayor of Boston refused to assign policemen to guard the building.

At a hearing held that afternoon, February 15, five respected Boston attorneys volunteered to defend Jenkins, asking for several days to prepare their case. As the courtroom was cleared, a crowd of blacks burst into the room, overpowered the deputy marshals, and escaped with Jenkins, cheered by a crowd that had gathered outside. The fugitive made his way to Canada, and the eight men who were arrested for their part in his escape, including four whites, also went free, the jury refusing to convict them.

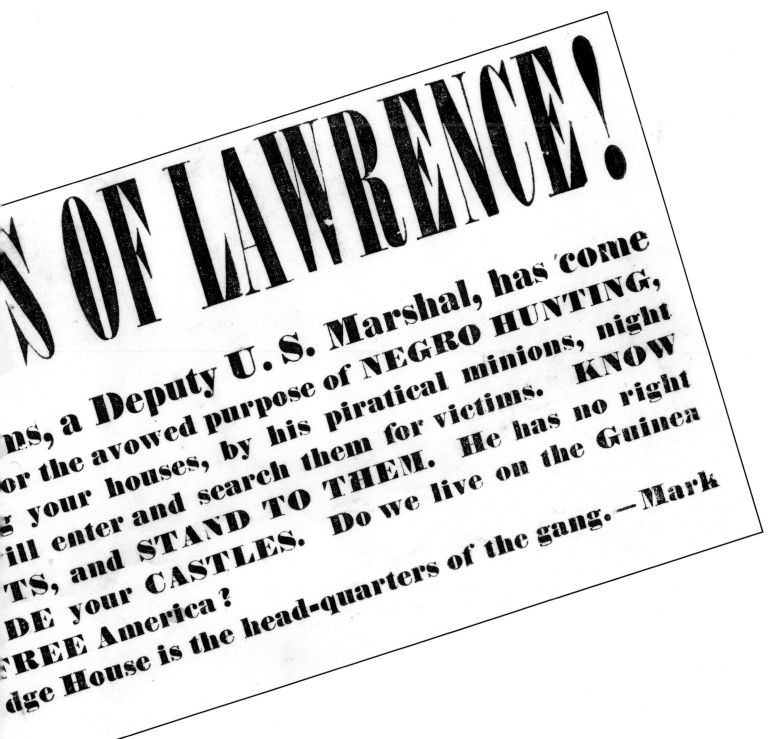

In May 1854 a Boston riot to free fugitive slave Anthony Burns resulted in the death of Deputy Marshal James Batchelder, who was shot as he tried to repel the assailants. Deputy Marshal A. P. Dayton of Oberlin, Ohio, was forcibly prevented from arresting two fugitive slaves on two occasions in the summer of 1858: like many other marshals charged with enforcing the hated Fugitive Slave Law, he was totally ostracized by his community. In Wisconsin, opposition to the marshals who arrested Sherman Booth, the leader of a fugitive-slave rescue in 1854, was so widespread that the Wisconsin Supreme Court refused to obey federal court orders after Booth was released from jail by armed supporters: perhaps only the fact that the marshals were soon able to recapture Booth prevented the situation from becoming a Constitutional crisis.

The portents were equally clear throughout the 1850s in the South, where local juries almost without fail refused to convict men arrested for their obvious involement in the African slave trade. Since attacks on the law in both the North and the South amounted to attacks on the government, it was clear that the Union itself was in deep disarray. The problem was not confined to specific areas such as "Bleeding Kansas" but was epidemic. As U.S. Attorney General Jeremiah Black wrote in 1859:

If the two sections of the Union will emulate one another in the violation of law and the impunity they give to criminals . . . it will not be very long before we cease to have any law at all.

BELOW: *Taunted by an angry crowd, Boston officers convey a recaptured slave to the harbor for shipment to Savannah, Georgia.*

RIGHT: *Deputy Marshal James Batchelder was killed in a Boston riot to free fugitive slave Anthony Burns in 1854.*

BELOW: *The brig* Acorn *leaves Boston Harbor with a fugitive slave in the custody of a U.S. marshal in 1851. Boston had long been a stronghold of abolitionism.*

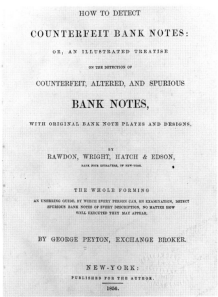

HOW TO DETECT

COUNTERFEIT BANK NOTES:

OR, AN ILLUSTRATED TREATISE

ON THE DETECTION OF

COUNTERFEIT, ALTERED, AND SPURIOUS

BANK NOTES,

WITH ORIGINAL BANK NOTE PLATES AND DESIGNS.

BY

RAWDON, WRIGHT, HATCH & EDSON,
BANK NOTE ENGRAVERS, OF NEW-YORK.

THE WHOLE FORMING

AN UNERRING GUIDE, BY WHICH EVERY PERSON CAN, ON EXAMINATION, DETECT
SPURIOUS BANK NOTES OF EVERY DESCRIPTION, NO MATTER HOW
WELL EXECUTED THEY MAY APPEAR.

BY GEORGE PEYTON, EXCHANGE BROKER.

NEW-YORK:

PUBLISHED FOR THE AUTHOR.

1856.

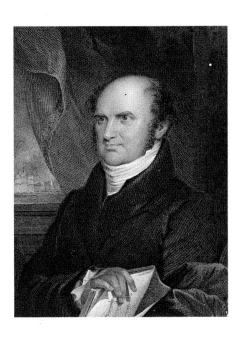

LEFT: The Counterfeiters, *an 1853 painting by Eastman Johnson.*

ABOVE: *Counterfeit bank notes were a major problem for Levi Woodbury, secretary of the treasury.*

The U.S. marshals faced two other challenges to federal authority during the years between 1815 and the outbreak of the Civil War in 1861. The first was widespread counterfeiting – an easy matter for skilled "coneymen," as they were called, because of the bewildering variety of currency in use at the time. Individual banks issued their own currency – bank notes – in all denominations, and the lack of regulation meant that many of the banks were unsound. The U.S. Mint manufactured primarily gold and silver coins until the Civil War: government paper currency included only denominations of less than $1.00, but Treasury notes and postal currency were also used as tender. Gold and silver coins issued by private banks added to the confusion. It has been estimated that one-third of the currency in circulation by 1860 was counterfeit.

The Treasury Department sometimes hired detectives as special agents to break up large counterfeiting rings, but for the most part it looked to the marshals. They became experts on the trade in bogus money, which was manufactured by printers and coiners, then sold to "passers," who exchanged the counterfeits for legitimate currency or goods. Ohio was a hotbed of counterfeiting, and Ohio Marshal Daniel A. Robertson and his deputies taught their colleagues in other states some useful lessons about how to handle the problem. By 1847 Marshal Robertson had compiled the names of some 50 successful counterfeiters, whom he pursued with tenacity. One of his principal targets was a gang led by a man named James Burns, who used his cover as a lecturer to circulate fake coins made from plaster molds.

Robertson's chief deputy in Cincinnati, D. K. Goodin, eventually amassed enough evidence to arrest the elusive Burns – if they could catch him. The chase led from Burns's home in Sciotoville to the Cincinnati docks, where the counterfeiter had disembarked from a riverboat to take cover on the remote Western Row. The pursuers found his hiding place and, in his absence, persuaded his wife, who was deeply involved in the counterfeiting ring, that they were fellow coneymen. She confided that Burns had escaped to Virginia, which required a special warrant, granted that same night by a local judge. Deputies Long and Hayman took up the pursuit with a posse of 10 men and tracked Burns to the mouth of Virginia's Big Sandy, where he had taken refuge with an associate named Mark Williams. When they called upon Burns to surrender, he tried to escape from the rear of the house, only to be arrested by the posse. The company returned to Cincinnati in triumph and to the envious applause of other American lawmen.

Not until 1865 did Congress recognize the need for special measures against counterfeiting by creating the Secret Service under the Secretary of the Treasury. But as Marshal Robertson had earlier remarked, "The pursuit of Counterfeiters is a peculiar branch of police not much understood," and it would be some years before the new agency would be prepared to cope with the widespread problem. Thus the marshals were obliged to go on helping with investigations and arrests until the Secret Service was capable of assuming full responsibility.

Another kind of challenge resulted from the fact that prior to the Civil War, American enthusiasm for emerging independence movements in nearby nations led to flagrant violations of the neutrality laws. Cuba's revolt against Spain inspired a number of invasions launched from the United States by bands of American mercenaries called filibusters, and other adventurers took an active part in the effort of the tiny Canadian guerrilla army called the Patriots to overthrow British rule in that country. Foreign rebels against other nations in the Western Hemisphere found ready support and sympathy in the United States, which became a kind of staging ground for revolts.

Even the federal government turned a blind eye to some of the filibusters' activities until 1817 and 1818, when Congress passed two neutrality laws under pressure from Spain and the other European powers. These laws, which forbade American assistance to the revolt of Spain's colonies in Latin America, were closely followed, in 1823, by the Monroe Doctrine, which opposed any future colonization or intervention in the sovereign states of the Western Hemisphere by European powers. The lines were now legally drawn, but the filibusters were not easy to discourage. In 1817 Rhode Island reported two violations of the new neutrality law and South Carolina, eight.

LEFT: *Patriot Army volunteers drill for their attack on British Canada in 1837.*

BELOW: *A Patriot Army encampment in the Province of Quebec.*

The U.S. marshals of northern New York, led by Nathaniel Garrow, had to cope with the 1837 Patriot Army invasion of Canada, which had active support in Buffalo and much of the surrounding region. The Patriots numbered fewer than a thousand, but what they lacked in manpower, they made up in zeal for ridding Canada of British control. The British minister in Washington made a strong protest about the fact that Patriot insurgents had encamped on Canada's Navy Island, in the Niagara River, and were being supplied by American sympathizers via steamship. Marshal Garrow reported to Secretary of State John Forsyth that American support for the Patriots was strong all along the New York border and that many weapons were being provided to the insurgents.

Within days of his arrival in Buffalo on December 23 Garrow realized that he and his two deputies could do little without military assistance, which he requested on December 28. This request was denied just as the situation became explosive, for at that point the American ship *Caroline*, which was supplying the Patriots on Navy Island, was attacked by Canadian militiamen who

had crossed the Niagara River. The Canadian militiamen not only set fire to the ship but also cast it adrift on the Niagara River not far above the falls. In the course of *Carolina*'s subsequent destruction an American named Amos Durfee was killed.

Marshal Garrow and his men harried the Patriots as best they could, until the Patriots finally took up a new position on Fighting Island, also outside U.S. jurisdiction. This was, however, the beginning of the end for the Patriots: their ordnance officer had surrendered to Marshal Garrow, and British forces subsequently invaded the island on February 25, 1838. Five men were killed on each side before the Patriots retreated across the frozen river to the American shore and dispersed into hiding, but their commanding general, William Lyon Mackenzie, was soon captured by the marshals. His adjutant, Donald MacLeod, fled into Michigan and eluded pursuit, but the Patriot cause fell apart that spring. U.S. marshals in Michigan and Ohio nevertheless kept the remnants of the Patriot Army and its sympathizers under surveillance for several years thereafter.

Westward expansion encouraged filibusters in several ways. The successful revolt of the Texans against Mexico and the subsequent Mexican War, in which vast new territories were acquired, fueled the ambition for still greater conquests. Mercenary expeditions held

LEFT: *In 1860 the government of Honduras arrested Walker for his military adventures in Central America, including Mexico and Nicaragua. A California court had tried Walker for violations of the neutrality laws in 1854 and acquitted him, but he was summarily executed by the Honduran government.*

out the promise of adventure and wealth. Spanish Cuba was the target of numerous invasions, including four led by Narciso López before he was finally captured and executed by Spanish authorities in 1851, after eluding U.S. marshals from New York City to New Orleans. Of the 424 filibusters involved in that expedition, more than a hundred were killed in battle or executed, and those who were captured languished in Spanish jails. The ill-fated expedition's resupply ship, *Pampero*, was blockaded on Florida's St. Johns River, near Jacksonville, until its crew and passengers surrendered.

During the 1850s the filibusters violated U.S. neutrality laws in such diverse locations as Mexico, Nicaragua, Ecuador, Guatemala, El Salvador, Costa Rica, Peru, and Honduras. The best-known filibuster of that turbulent decade was William Walker, who was arrested by the marshals several times, only to be released by sympathetic juries. The length of America's coastline, and the many hiding places it afforded, made it nearly impossible for officials to stop the embarrassing filibustering expeditions.

Walker's career was finally cut short by a Honduran firing squad in 1860, after he had conquered and ruled Nicaragua for more than a year before being expelled in 1857. But by the time of his death adventures abroad had lost their appeal: Americans were now turning to the somber business of civil war.

Civil War and Reconstruction

U.S. Marshal Ward Hill Lamon, a friend of President Abraham Lincoln for 20 years, was present at the creation of the Civil War. As a bodyguard he accompanied the president-elect to Washington, D.C., for his inauguration on March 4, 1861, and soon afterward received his commission as U.S. marshal for the District of Columbia.

The capital was gripped by tension. South Carolina had declared its secession from the Union on December 20, 1860, two months after Lincoln's election. Union forces under Major Robert Anderson were besieged in Fort Sumter, in Charleston harbor, having refused

BELOW: *Abraham Lincoln's appointment of Levi J. Keithley as U.S. marshal for the Territory of New Mexico.*

ABOVE: *Lincoln's friend Ward Hill Lamon, second from left, was U.S. marshal for the District of Columbia when he accompanied the president into the field in October 1862.*

to comply with South Carolina's demand that they evacuate the fort and return to the North. Marshal Lamon traveled to Charleston at the end of March in an effort to defuse the situation at Fort Sumter, but his mission failed. Early on the morning of April 12 South Carolina forces began to bombard the fort. Thirty-four hours later, Major Anderson surrendered.

As one Southern state after another seceded from the Union, almost all the U.S. marshals in the Southern judicial districts resigned their commissions, and marshals in the Western states and territories struggled against strong secessionist movements in California, Arizona, and New Mexico Territories. A southern California marshal, Henry D. Barrows, reported to Attorney General Edward Bates in September 1961:

> Treason is rampant here in Southern California . . . We have bold daring Secessionists who are plotting in secret; our Sheriff and nearly all our county officers just elected disavow all allegiance to our Government and say that Jeff Davis' government is the only Constitutional government! And there *must be collision.*

33

The situation was even worse in such border states as Maryland and Missouri, where Confederate sympathizers sabotaged Union troop movements, smuggled goods and arms into the South, and acted as spies from the war's earliest days.

The marshals' principal wartime duties were to arrest suspected traitors and Confederate sympathizers and to confiscate property being used to support the insurrection. Many of the arrests were made at the request of local military commanders rather than by court order, and the right of habeas corpus was suspended over the objections of Supreme Court Chief Justice Roger B. Taney: prisoners accused of treason or conspiracy lost the right to hear the charges against them in open court.

Attorney General Bates did the best he could for the marshals of the Union states, but they often faced opposition to their arrests of suspected traitors and Confederate sympathizers. When New Jersey Marshal Benajah Deacon arrested two men who had actively discouraged enlistment in the Union Army in 1862, the judge advocate of the local troops released them within four days of taking custody. In Illinois, a county circuit court indicted Marshal David L. Phillips for kidnapping and criminal trespass after he arrested three suspected traitors in 1863. Marshal Barrows of southern California was sued for false imprisonment by a Confederate sympathizer whom he had arrested. Local loyalty, even in the courts, often took precedence over the national emergency.

The confiscation acts of 1861 and 1862 gave the marshals broad authority to seize personal property that was believed to be used for the benefit and support of the South. They were also empowered to take title to real property in such cases, but only to prevent its sale, not to evict its owners. (Marshal James T. Close of Alexandria, Virginia, lost his post when he exceeded his authority by actually taking possession of several houses in this jurisdiction, rather than seizing the titles.) The government's power to confiscate remained in force until 1868, but by that time the U.S. marshals had even thornier problems to deal with. After the war ended in 1865, it fell to them to reimpose federal authority on the embittered South and to protect millions of freed slaves, now citizens, from their former owners.

Late in 1865 Confederate veterans in Pulaski, Tennessee, formed a secret organization that soon became a widespread agent of terrorism against black freedmen and their families. Calling themselves the Ku Klux Klan, the veterans rode out at night disguised in white robes and hoods and brandishing weapons to frighten blacks who tried to exercise their rights of citizenship. Under various names, including the White League and the Georgia Army, such groups spread rapidly through the South in defiance of the Civil Rights Act of 1866, and it was not long before the Klansmen's threats turned to outright violence.

LEFT: *Chief Justice Roger B. Taney objected to the suppression of the right of habeas corpus during the Civil War, but he was overruled. Persons accused of conspiracy or treason against the Union lost the right to hear the charges against them in open court.*

BOTTOM RIGHT: *An exposé of crimes committed by the Ku Klux Klan during the Reconstruction era in the South.*

BELOW: *Klan terrorists threaten a freedman's household.*

When former Union commander Ulysses S. Grant succeeded the more lenient President Andrew Johnson in 1868, white Southerners redoubled their efforts to regain political control of their states by any means, and by 1871 they had done so in Georgia, North Carolina, Tennessee, and Virginia. The Klan (or Force) acts of 1870 and 1871 put U.S. marshals and deputies in charge of supervising every polling place for Congressional elections in the nation's cities in an effort to stop the violence against politically active blacks. New legislation was directed specifically against the Klan and similar organizations, making it a federal crime to wear masks or disguises and to attack any citizen on the basis of race, color, or previous condition of servitude. Not only would violators of the laws be tried in federal court, the president could impose martial law and suspend the right of habeas corpus in places where terrorism was rampant.

With the help of the army, Southern marshals made mass arrests of Klansmen throughout the former Confederate States: some 7,000 Southerners were arrested for violations of the civil rights laws between the late 1860s and 1877, when the period of Radical

Reconstruction ended. Marshal J. H. Pierce of Mississippi well expressed the marshals' commitment when he said in 1871:

> My heart is enlisted in the cause of putting down lawlessness and restoring order by enforcing the laws that every man, even the most humble citizen of the land, may feel that his life and property are safe, and that he can express his loyalty and give his support to the government and its officers without fear of being deprived of his life.

That same year, Mississippi Deputy C. H. Wisler was murdered during the trial of Klansmen whom he had arrested. Four other Southern deputies lost their lives in enforcing the civil rights laws over the next three years.

Shortly after the election of 1872, which was marked by violence in many districts, a group of whites in Grant Parish, Louisiana, attacked more than a hundred freedmen who claimed victory in the election. The blacks were pinned down in the Colfax courthouse by relentless rifle fire, with little chance to use their weapons. Most of them were massacred, and 20 men who were taken prisoner were shot that same night.

The U.S. attorney for Louisiana, J. R. Beckwith, obtained 72 indictments against the perpetrators, but the attorney general declined to send soldiers into Grant Parish to back up Marshal Stephen B. Packard in making the arrests. Rightly fearing armed resistance to arrest, Packard called upon the state's governor for militia troops. Despite lack of support from the Grant administration, which had prematurely decided that the worst Klan-type terrorism in the South was over, Packard pursued his investigations for a year and arrested 9 of the 72 men who had been indicted. Their first trial ended in a hung jury and their second in only four convictions. Those found guilty appealed successfully to the Supreme Court in the name of defendant William B. Cruikshank. In fact, the 1876 decision in *U.S. v. Cruikshank et al.* dismantled most of the protection the federal government had extended to freedmen by finding major portions of the Klan acts unconstitutional. The Court denied that the federal government had the power to protect "private citizens" and their rights from one another and referred the prosecution of such crimes as the Colfax courthouse massacre to the states.

The 1876 election of Rutherford B. Hayes to the presidency confirmed the fact that the freedmen – and the marshals who protected them – were now on their own. In the disputed election, Hayes had obtained the votes of Louisiana, Georgia, and Florida in exchange for a promise to withdraw federal troops throughout the South, thus breaking a deadlock in the electoral college and winning the presidency. Hayes's subsequent appointment of two prominent

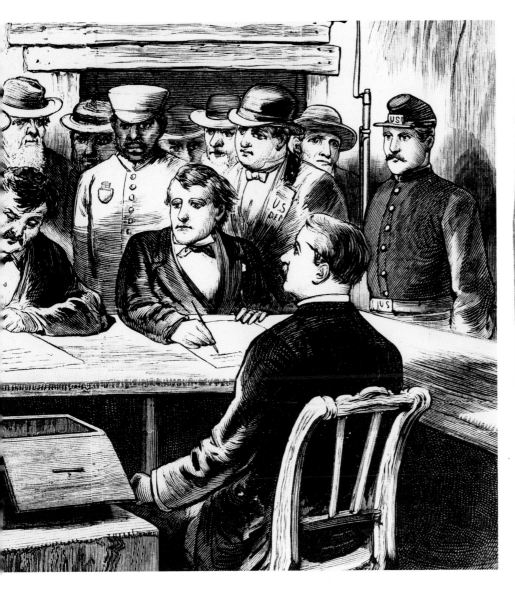

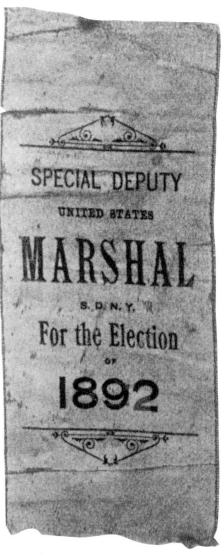

ABOVE: *U.S. deputy marshals, identified by ribbons, oversee a tally of election results in the postwar South.*

TOP RIGHT: *A deputy marshal's ribbon from the election of 1892 in New York's Southern District.*

LEFT: *A political cartoon depicting the U.S. marshal's office as protector of the black freedman against Southern racism.*

blacks to high federal office did nothing to improve the situation: he named abolitionist and activist Frederick Douglass the marshal for the District of Columbia and appointed former U. S. Marshal Charles Devens the new attorney general, but both wanted an end to Reconstruction, despite their personal sympathy for the freedmen of the South and their protectors.

The federal government took a much stronger line with evaders of the revenue tax on whisky in the Moonshine Wars that broke out in the South in the 1870s – about the same time that U.S. marshals were being denied the right to call on help from the U.S. Army in cases of racist violence. In a reprise of the Whisky Rebellion of 1794, Southern distillers refused to pay the 90-cent excise tax that had been imposed on whisky during the Civil War. Called moonshiners because they worked by night in remote areas, the men who owned the stills, with the tacit support of their friends and neighbors, posed a serious threat to federal revenuers and the deputy marshals who accompanied them into the often-remote and always-hostile countryside to help them make arrests.

FAR RIGHT: *A late 19th-century sketch entitled* U.S. Deputy Marshals Surprising a "Moonshiner."

RIGHT: *Abolitionist Frederick Douglass.*

In Greenville, South Carolina, Deputy Marshal Rufus Springs was shot from ambush during a raid on moonshiners in early 1878. He and his party, including Internal Revenue officer H. H. Gillson, had already destroyed four illegal stills in the vicinity, and they were aware of the danger. While Gillson smashed the barrels of whisky in the newly abandoned stillhouse, where embers of a fire still burned, Springs reconnoitered the nearby woods. When he returned to the stillhouse, he was cut down by a rifle shot from the woods. The rest of the revenuers were pursued for several miles as they fled back to Greenville with the deputy's body, which had been hastily tied to the back of his horse.

Southern resistance to the national tax on whisky was far more virulent than that in other regions because of the enduring legacy of bitterness from the Civil War. Many officers were reluctant to go into the mountainous country of the Carolinas, Alabama, and Virginia in search of illegal stills. Marshal Robert M. Wallace of South Carolina reported that attacks on his deputies were commonplace in the late 1870s. In North Carolina two deputies had been killed and others wounded by 1877. The violence continued well into the 1880s, with at last 36 deputy marshals killed in the line of duty. For the marshals and the revenuers, it was civil war all over again, with little support from the federal government and less from state and local authorities. Americans had always resented taxes on their whisky, and they would continue do to so into the 20th century. But not until Prohibition was enacted in 1919 would so many federal officers lose their lives in trying to enforce a measure that was almost unenforceable.

Moving West with the Frontier

As the restless American people moved westward, the U.S. marshals went with them to uphold the law in remote, sparsely populated, unorganized territories. They were not the only peace officers on the frontier, but as representatives of the federal government, they were highest in rank. Thus they received both cooperation and opposition from other lawmen within their jurisdictions.

Each frontier town chose its own marshal – effectively, the chief of police – who usually headed a small force that included an assistant town marshal and a handful of policemen. Ordinary citizens could be pressed into service in case of emergency, and sometimes they took the law into their own hands as lynch mobs and vigilantes. Self-reliance was the watchword of the frontier, and every man carried a gun.

CENTER: *The marshal's badge identified the preeminent peace officer in the sprawling new territories of the frontier West.*

LEFT: *Frontier justice for an accused murderer is meted out by a lynch mob.*

TOP: *A Frederic Remington woodcut depicting a barroom brawl in a Wild West saloon.*

On the county level, law enforcement was the job of a sheriff, who got help from some regular deputy sheriffs and ad hoc posses when the situation demanded it, which was often. Cattle towns, mining towns, railroad towns and counties attracted a plethora of rootless men with little to lose, from professional gamblers to trail-weary cowboys looking for excitement. They got drunk at the local saloon and "hurrahed" through town on horseback, firing their six-shooters into the air and sometimes into each other and innocent bystanders. Camp followers and other prostitutes were readily available and were frequent occasions for conflict between drunken men who were far from civilization and its restraints.

After the Civil War many former Confederate guerrillas left the desolate South in anger and despair, to become bank, train, and stagecoach robbers who killed with impunity. Among the most famous of these were Frank and Jesse James. The brothers became gang leaders and outlaws in 1866, when they entered the Clay County Savings Association in Liberty, Missouri, and demanded "all the money in the bank" after asking for change of a ten-dollar bill.

As they fled the town with $60,000 in legal tender, they shot down a 19-year-old college student who was running for cover. He died instantly from four bullet wounds, any one of which would have been fatal. Furious townspeople tracked the gang to a Missouri River ferry crossing, but a winter storm forced the posse to turn back. Meanwhile, just a little north of Liberty, the James brothers had gone to ground at their ramshackle home in Kearney, owned by their mother, the former widow James, who had remarried.

For all the citizens of Kearney knew, the James boys were resting up from their Civil War service at the farmhouse. It was believed that 19-year-old Jesse, the younger by three years, was recovering from a battle wound and that the bookish Frank was neglecting his chores in favor of reading. The fact that the brothers had become leaders of an outlaw gang, with an ever-changing cast of

LEFT: *Frank James (center) and his brother James (right) with Confederate comrade Fletch Taylor during the Civil War.*

ABOVE: *Train and stagecoach robbery usually involved the U.S. mails, which sent the marshals after the James brothers.*

TOP RIGHT: *The James gang and its exploits were featured in the 1890s magazine* Detective Library.

RIGHT: *The widow James and her boys.*

LEFT: *Jesse James was gunned down by gang member Bob Ford in 1882. James was considered a war hero by fellow citizens of Missouri.*

BELOW: *James Butler (Wild Bill) Hickok had a colorful career as a Union scout during the Civil War and as a U.S. marshal in the postwar West.*

desperadoes, did not become known until four years later, after "the boys" had committed their sixth bank robbery. Their criminal career would last for 15 years – the longest by far of any outlaw gang of the Old West, and the most famous. During that time they would rob 12 banks, seven trains, and five stages in 11 states and territories and be pursued by town marshals, county sheriffs, Pinkerton detectives, Missouri State secret agents, and U.S. marshals. The U.S. marshals were involved because the federal mails were being robbed, especially in train and stagecoach hold-ups, which were a specialty of the James brothers. They were never caught: in the end, Frank turned himself in to the governor of Missouri after Jesse was shot in the back by gang member Bob Ford.

Public sentiment in Missouri had always favored the James boys as Civil War heroes, despite their many crimes, and an Independence jury refused to convict Frank of murder in the death of a passenger during a train robbery. He retired into

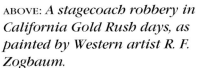

ABOVE: *A stagecoach robbery in California Gold Rush days, as painted by Western artist R. F. Zogbaum.*

semirespectability and lived to the age of 82, charging admission to his birthplace, James Farm, and selling pebbles from Jesse's grave to visiting tourists.

In dying of natural causes Frank James was an exception to the outlaw rule. Many gang members died violently, in shoot-outs with lawmen or one another, and most of the rest ended up on the gallows. In unorganized territory the marshals were the only lawmen and, effectively, the only law. When a vagrant named Jack McCall shot James Butler (Wild Bill) Hickok in Deadwood, Dakota Territory, in 1876, the townspeople convened an ad hoc court and sentenced McCall to hang. His attorneys appealed the case, on grounds that Deadwood was in the unorganized part of Dakota Territory and that therefore its citizens had no power to form a court or to try, convict, or execute their client. The killer had a year's reprieve before federal officials, including deputy marshals, could form a legal court, re-find him guilty, and hang him according to the book.

Even local peace officers were sometimes hamstrung by the casual nature of arrangements for law enforcement. When the town of Ellsworth, Kansas, got its charter in 1871, the mayor and town council rushed to appoint a marshal to enforce the community's laws — then realized that they had never passed any laws for him to uphold. It was a week before this oversight could be remedied.

Even with laws on the books, however, keeping order on the frontier was a precarious business at best. Often, the U.S. marshal and his deputies were the court of last resort. In federal matters, such as safe delivery of the U.S. mails, protection of the Indians, and safeguarding of government property, they were the only resort.

A hodgepodge of federal laws had been contrived to isolate the eastern Indians, called the Five Civilized Tribes, on reservations whose boundaries kept shrinking and moving west with the frontier. In 1830 the Indian Removal Act had provided for the removal of these five tribes – the Cherokee, Choctaw, Chickasaw, Creek, and Seminole – to lands west of the Mississippi River. Five years earlier, Indian Territory had been created for this purpose when Congress approved a frontier line that blocked off all of present-day Oklahoma as Indian land not open to settlement. But year by year, through purchases, treaties whose provisions were not honored by the government, and outright land grabs, Indian Territory was encroached upon by land-hungry homesteaders in the Mississippi Valley Basin. Thus things continued to get worse, not only for the Indians but for the relative handful of U.S. deputy marshals who were charged with protecting them from rapacious whites.

The marshals' base was Western District of Arkansas headquarters in Fort Smith, a drab, dusty settlement that did a thriving business in saloons frequented by itinerant cowboys, traders, railroad men, and

LEFT: *A caricature of the Cherokee Nation overwhelmed by political land grabs, railroad interests, and broken government promises.*

BELOW: *Almost 2 million acres of Oklahoma Territory formerly owned by the Creek and Seminole tribes was opened to settlement at noon on April 22, 1889. The marshals and the army arrested claim-jumpers, called Sooners, who entered the territory before the appointed time.*

the riverboat crews that plied the Mississippi and its tributaries. Just across the Arkansas River from Fort Smith was Indian Territory and the fifty-mile strip adjacent to it known as No Man's Land – the two most violent territories in the nation. Most whites who entered the unorganized territory prior to the Oklahoma land rush of 1889 were drifters, thieves, and fugitives of the most desperate kind, and during the 1870s some 200 deputy marshals patrolled 74,000 square miles of Indian Territory. A set of instructions issued by the U.S. Marshal's Office in Fort Smith gives an idea of their problems:

U.S. Deputy Marshals for the Western District of Arkansas may make arrests for: murder, manslaughter, assault with intent to kill or to maim, attempts to murder, arson, robbery, rape, bribery, burglary, larceny, incest, adultery . . . . These arrests may be made with or without warrant first issued and in the hands of the Deputy or the Chief Marshal . . . . For violations of the revenue law and for introducing ardent spirits into the Indian Country, the Deputy can not make an arrest without warrant unless the offender is caught in the act.

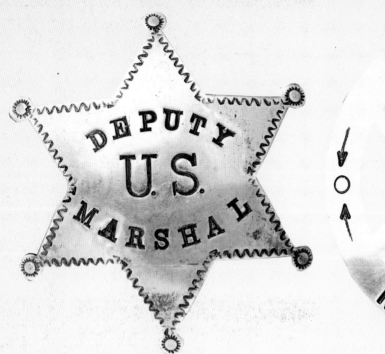

BELOW: *A document appointing six deputy marshals for the Wyoming Territory, signed by Marshal J. P. Rankin in 1892.*

TOP LEFT AND ABOVE: *Deputy marshal badges of the 1880s, 60 years before the first standard-issue badge for the service came into use.*

ABOVE RIGHT: *A sheet-silver badge engraved and hallmarked by Best Stamp Company.*
RIGHT: *Texas deputies patrolled the dangerous Mexican border.*

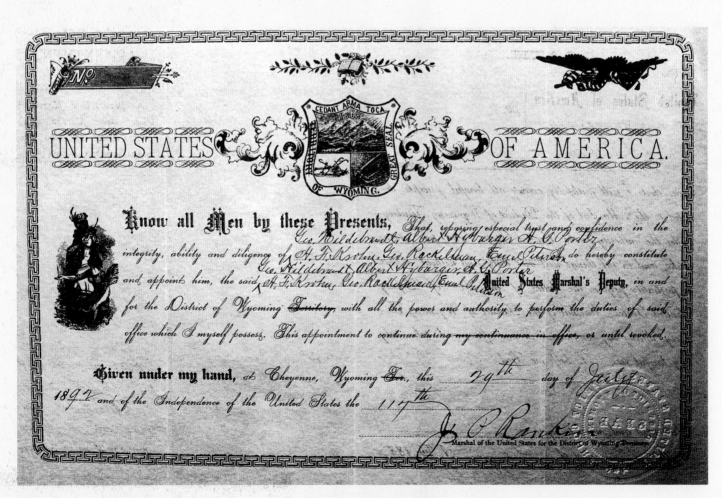

LEFT: *Oklahoma Territory marshals oversaw a vast tract of conflict-ridden wilderness.*

U. S. Marshal's Office,
Western District of Arkansas,
Fort Smith, Arkansas.

LAWS

GOVERNING U. S. MARSHAL

...... AND ......

His Deputies.

U. S. Deputy Marshals for the Western District of Arkansas
may make arrests for
MURDER, MANSLAUGHTER,
ASSAULT, WITH INTENT TO KILL OR TO MAIM,
ATTEMPTS TO MURDER,
ARSON, ROBBERY, RAPE, BURGLARY,
LARCENY, INCEST, ADULTERY,
WILFULLY AND MALICIOUSLY PLACING OBSTRUCTIONS
ON A RAILROAD TRACK.

These arrests may be made with or without warrant first issued and in the hands of the Deputy or the Chief Marshal. It is always better for the Deputy to have a warrant before making an arrest, yet if he knows of any one of the above crimes having been committed and has good reason to believe a particular party guilty of the crime, his duty is to make the arrest.

For violations of the revenue law and for introducing ardent spirits into the Indian Country, the Deputy can not make an arrest without warrant, unless the offender is caught in the act, when he can arrest for these offenses without a warrant. The Deputy can arrest for violations of the revenue law, the intercourse law and the laws of the United States against counterfeiting, and for violations of the postal laws, or for larceny of the property of the United States, when any of these offenses are committed by an Indian. Also when an assault with intent to kill or maim, a murder, or manslaughter has been committed by an Indian upon an Indian Agent, Indian Policeman, Indian United States Deputy Marshal or guard or any person at any time while in the discharge of duty or at any time

RIGHT: *Marshals for the Indian Territory, based in Fort Smith, Arkansas, were empowered to make arrests without warrant when necessary.*

Naturally, "ardent spirits" and weapons continued to reach the Indians despite the provisions of what was called the Intercourse Act. And as the Indians' share of the prairie continued to shrink, they became increasingly prone to outbursts of violence against white settlers and traders. Crimes among Indians were supposed to be resolved by Indian tribunals, but those involving Indians and whites were dealt with by the marshals. Ambiguity on both sides and the murkiness of the legal situation were bound to cause trouble in the territory. The worst such incident was the Going Snake Massacre of 1872.

Early in 1872 a Cherokee named Proctor shot and wounded a white man named Kecterson and killed his Indian wife. The Cherokee court charged Proctor with the woman's murder, but her husband was afraid the assailant would be acquitted. Kecterson applied to the U.S. commissioner for a federal warrant against Proctor for assaulting him, and an arrest warrant was issued to Deputy Marshals Jacob Owens and Joseph Peavy. Their instructions were to serve the warrant only if the Cherokee district court did not convict Proctor of murder.

With a posse of 10 men, Owens and Peavy reached the Going Snake Cherokee district court on April 15 and found that the court had convened at a local schoolhouse rather than its usual venue. The setting was readily defensible, and the Cherokees were armed. Among the posse were four relatives of the murdered woman, and the Indians assumed that the deputies had come with intentions hostile to Proctor. Deputy Owens had instructed his men to take their seats at the back of the court and wait for the verdict. It is unclear whether the deputies drew their weapons upon approaching the courthouse or not, but as the marshals crossed the clearing, several Cherokees came outside and fired into the possee. In the ensuing melee seven deputies were killed as they tried to retreat, and Deputy Owens was mortally wounded. It was the largest loss of life in the history of the marshals. The lawmen killed three Indians and wounded six others. Not surprisingly, the following day the Cherokee court acquitted Proctor of the murder.

When Cherokee Ned Christie left his tribe and his trade as a gunsmith to wage war on white settlers, he became the target of an 1892 manhunt led by Deputy Marshal Paden Tolbert. Christie robbed trains, killed, stole horses, and peddled whisky in the Cherokees' northeastern domain until he was tracked to Rabbit Trap Canyon, near the town of Tahlequah. There Christie and another Indian outlaw, Archie Wolf, had built a log fort high on the

RIGHT: *Ten of the deputy marshals at Fort Smith, Arkansas, in the late 1880s.*

LEFT: *Cherokee outlaw Ned Christie, killed by a 16-man posse led by Deputy Marshal Paden Tolbert in 1892. Christie was wanted for crimes including murder, train robbery, and horse theft.*

rim of the canyon. The two were trapped by the 16-man posse below, but they refused to surrender and returned the lawmen's fire. It took six sticks of dynamite to dislodge Christie and his partner from their burning stronghold. Archie Wolf made his escape, but Christie was killed in a hail of gunfire.

In most cases, deputy marshals did not shoot to kill or travel with large posses. Their usual practice was to go out "on the scout" in groups of four or five, with a wagon that could double as a jail when arrests were made. They looked for stolen horses, for suspicious travelers, for stills and contraband whisky, and for wanted men on the run. Paid at the rate of six cents per mile traveled and two dollars per arrest, they were lucky to clear $500 a year. And their progress back to Fort Smith with prisoners for trial was often slowed by the presence of reluctant witnesses who had to be coerced to make the long trip back across the Arkansas River.

Despite these limitations, conscientious deputy marshals such as Heck Thomas, Bill Tilghman, and Chris Madsen — known as the Three Guardsmen of Oklahoma — did much to curb the disorder rampant in Indian Territory. They pursued such notorious criminals as gang leader Bill Doolin, Indian outlaw Rufus Buck, and Belle Starr, who was a successful bootlegger and dealt in stolen livestock. Belle had a penchant for criminal lovers like Cole Younger (a member of the James gang and leader, with his three brothers, of the Younger Gang), Cherokee bandit Sam Starr, the desperado known as Blue Duck, and horse thief Jim Reed. She married Sam Starr and helped plan their criminal activities from a hideout on the Canadian River, west of Fort Smith. When these plans finally went awry she tried to seduce or bribe the deputy marshals who took her associates into custody. Failing that, she appealed to President Grover Cleveland on two occasions through expensive lawyers dispatched to Washington. When Blue Duck was convicted of murder in the federal court at Fort Smith, and sentenced to hang by the dreaded judge Isaac C. Parker, she managed to get his sentence commuted to life imprisonment. Her second appeal to the White House, on behalf of her son — a horse thief who took after his father, Jim Reed — resulted in a full pardon. Parker deeply resented these challenges to his authority, but there was little he could do about it.

The man who became known as "the Hanging Judge" was a 36-year-old former Congressman from Missouri when, in 1875, President Ulysses S. Grant appointed him federal judge for the hard-pressed Western District of Arkansas. Parker had actually volunteered for the job, which no one else wanted, and the government was quick to send him into the troublesome territory. During his 21-year tenure at Fort Smith, fraught with controversy, he would send hundreds of outlaws to prison and sentence 160 men to death. Of these, 79 would be executed by deputy marshals on the Fort Smith gallows.

ABOVE: *Cherokee bandit Sam Starr, aka Blue Duck, and wife Belle.*

RIGHT: *Belle Starr's exploits included bootlegging and livestock rustling from her hideout on the Canadian River, west of Fort Smith.*

OPPOSITE TOP LEFT: *A deputy's personalized silver pin, combining star and crescent.*

CLOCKWISE FROM TOP RIGHT: *Deputy Marshals Chris Madsen and Heck Thomas, and Marshal Bill Tilghman: the legendary Three Guardsmen of Oklahoma.*

In his zeal to curb crime in Indian Territory, Parker sometimes hired dubious candidates for deputy marshal on the strength of their skill with a gun. Some of these men eventually turned to crime themselves, including two of the Dalton brothers. But the majority of Parker's recruits were honest, hard-working lawmen, 65 of whom died in the line of duty. Parker's orders were to "Bring them in alive – or dead."

The relentless Parker did not spare himself in the daily struggle to keep pace with a constant backlog of prisoners and witnesses. He held court from eight-thirty in the morning until dark, six days a week, and then usually walked home alone (at no small risk to his life). But in fact, the case load at Fort Smith – which included 30 Arkansas counties besides the Indian Territory – had always been too heavy for a single court, and in 1883 Congress removed the western half of Indian Territory from Parker's jurisdiction and divided it between the nearest district courts in Kansas and Texas. Six years later Congress finally took steps to limit Parker's unique authority to impose the death penalty without the possibility of the convict's appeal to the U.S. Supreme Court. (Prior to that his decisions could not be challenged, although convicted criminals in other jurisdictions could appeal.) Parker, of course, felt that this undermined his power to keep crime in the Indian Territory under control, and there was no doubt that he did want to protect the Indians under his jurisdiction from exploitation. When the Oklahoma "Boomers" and "Sooners" made their run into the territory's Unassigned Lands in 1889, he was one of the few to protest bitterly that the government had once again contrived to betray the Indians.

In 1890 all of Indian Territory, except for lands owned by the Five Civilized Tribes, was established as the Oklahoma Territory, with its own government and court system. But both the Twin Territories, as they were called, would remain havens for outlaws of every kind throughout the 1890s and into the twentieth century.

ABOVE: *The court of Isaac Parker, "the Hanging Judge," at Fort Smith, Arkansas, where 79 criminals died on the gallows.*

BELOW: *Detective Allan Pinkerton, who did secret service work for the Union Army during the Civil War, later joined Western marshals in the pursuit of several outlaws.*

Overlap of jurisdiction was often a source of conflict between territorial and federal lawmen. What made it even more confusing was the fact that many sheriffs and town marshals also held commissions as federal deputy marshals. The federal marshals often clashed with local peace officers and sometimes took sides in local disputes. This was the case in New Mexico's Lincoln County War of 1878–79. U.S. Marshal John Sherman sent Deputy Robert Widenmann into Lincoln County to arrest the suspected killers of an Englishman named John Tunstall, who had been the victim of a power struggle between rival cattlemen James J. Dolan and John S. Chisum for control of the county. Deputy Widenmann made the mistake of allying himself with the Chisum faction. One of several unfortunate results of this decision was his acquisition from the Chisum ranch of a young posseman named William Bonney, who would be widely known as Billy the Kid during his brief but bloody career in crime.

Widenmann and his posse spent several months scouting the countryside for Tunstall's killers and being shot at by members of the Dolan faction. Several men were killed, including Deputy Marshal William Brady. The situation finally went out of control when the territorial governor allied himself with the Dolan group, and the federal government had to send the army in to pacify Lincoln County and fire the governor.

By this time Billy the Kid had gunned down two prisoners suspected of murder who had been promised safe conduct to the town of Lincoln. When the county war ended, Billy went on a three-year crime spree of rustling, robbery, and multiple murder, including that of three deputy marshals. He was finally shot by Deputy Marshal Pat Garrett, who was also the sheriff of Lincoln County. Garrett's fanciful account of the Kid's career, published in 1882, did much to further the legend that grew up around the youthful killer and, of course, around Garrett himself. He went on to serve in the Texas Rangers, then retired to ranching in New Mexico.

REWARD
($5,000.00)

Reward for the capture, dead or alive, of one Wm. Wright, better known as

"BILLY THE KID"

Age, 18. Height, 5 feet, 3 inches. Weight, 125 lbs. Light hair, blue eyes and even features. He is the leader of the worst band of desperadoes the Territory has ever had to deal with. The above reward will be paid for his capture or positive proof of his death.

JIM DALTON, Sheriff.

DEAD OR ALIVE!
"BILLY THE KID"

ABOVE: *Billy the Kid's trail of violence through New Mexico Territory in the late 1870s put a high price on his head.*

ABOVE: *Pat Garrett, deputy marshal and sheriff of Lincoln County, New Mexico, shot Billy the Kid after he escaped from jail in 1881 and killed two deputies.*

RIGHT: *The debonair Garrett became famous with his colorful account of the youthful outlaw's career, published in 1882.*

LEFT: *Bill Bonney was an itinerant ranch hand when he became involved in the Lincoln County War at the age of nineteen.*

Pinkerton's National Detective Agency.

FOUNDED BY ALLAN PINKERTON, 1850.

ROBT. A. PINKERTON, New York,	GEO. D. BANGS. General Manager, New York.	**OFFICES.**
WM. A. PINKERTON, Chicago.	ALLAN PINKERTON, Assistant General Manager, New York.	DENVER, OPERA HOUSE BLOCK. J. C. FRASER, Sup't.

Principals.

JOHN CORNISH, Gen'l Sup't., Eastern Division, New York.
EDWARD S. GAYLOR, Gen'l Sup't., Middle Division, Chicago.
JAMES McPARLAND, Gen'l Supt., Western Division, Denver.

NEW YORK, ST. BROADWAY
BOSTON, 30 COURT STREET
PHILADELPHIA, 441 CHESTNUT STREET
MONTREAL, MERCHANTS BANK BUILDING.
CHICAGO, 201 FIFTH AVENUE
ST. PAUL, GERMANIA BANK BUILDING
ST. LOUIS, WAINWRIGHT BUILDING
KANSAS CITY, 622 MAIN STREET
PORTLAND, ORE. WARQUAM BLOCK
SEATTLE, WASH BAILEY BLOCK
SAN FRANCISCO. CROCKER BUILDING

Attorneys: GUTHRIE, CRAVATH & HENDERSON. New York.

TELEPHONE CONNECTION.

REPRESENTING THE AMERICAN BANKERS' ASSOCIATION.

$4,000.00 REWARD.

CIRCULAR No. 2.

DENVER, Colo., January 24th, 1902.

THE FIRST NATIONAL BANK OF WINNEMUCCA, Nevada, a member of THE AMERICAN BANKERS' ASSOCIATION, was robbed of $32,640 at the noon hour, September 19th, 1900, by three men who entered the bank and "held up" the cashier and four other persons. Two of the robbers carried revolvers and a third a Winchester rifle. They compelled the five persons to go into the inner office of the bank while the robbery was committed.

At least $31,000 was in $20 gold coin; $1,200 in $5 and $10 gold coin; the balance in currency, including one $50 bill.

Since the issuance of our first circular, dated Denver, Colo., May 15th, 1901, it has been positively determined that two of the men who committed this robbery were:

1. GEORGE PARKER, alias "BUTCH" CASSIDY, alias GEORGE CASSIDY, alias INGERFIELD.
2. HARRY LONGBAUGH, alias "KID" LONGBAUGH, alias HARRY ALONZO, alias "THE SUNDANCE KID."

PARKER and LONGBAUGH are members of the HARVEY LOGAN alias "KID" CURRY band of bank and train (express) "hold up" robbers.

For the arrest, detention and surrender to an authorized officer of the State of Nevada of each or any one of the men who robbed the FIRST NATIONAL BANK OF WINNEMUCCA, the following rewards are offered:

BY THE FIRST NATIONAL BANK OF WINNEMUCCA: $1,000 for each robber.

Also 25 per cent., in proportionate shares, on all money recovered.

BY THE AMERICAN BANKERS' ASSOCIATION: $1,000 for each robber.

This reward to be paid on proper identification of either PARKER or LONGBAUGH.

Persons furnishing information leading to the arrest of either or all of the robbers will be entitled to share in the reward.

The outlaws, whose photographs, descriptions and histories appear on this circular MAY ATTEMPT TO CIRCULATE or be in possession of the following described NEW INCOMPLETE BANK NOTES of the NATIONAL BANK OF MONTANA and THE AMERICAN NATIONAL BANK, both of HELENA, MONT., which were stolen by members of the HARVEY LOGAN, alias "KID" CURRY BAND, from the GREAT NORTHERN (RAILWAY) EXPRESS No. 3, near Wagner, Mont., July 3rd, 1901, by "hold up" methods.

$40,000. INCOMPLETE NEW BANK NOTES of the NATIONAL BANK OF MONTANA (Helena, Montana), $24,000 of which was in ten dollar bills and $16,000 of which was in twenty dollar bills.

Serial Number 1201 to 2000 inclusive;
Government Number-Y 934349 to 935148 inclusive;
Charter Number 5671.

$500. INCOMPLETE BANK NOTES of AMERICAN NATIONAL BANK (Helena, Montana), $300 of which was in ten dollar bills and $200 of which was in twenty dollar bills.

Serial Number 3423 to 3432 inclusive;
Government Number V-662761 to V-662770 inclusive;
Charter Number 4396.

THESE INCOMPLETE BANK NOTES LACKED THE SIGNATURES OF THE PRESIDENTS AND CASHIERS OF THE BANKS NAMED, AND MAY BE CIRCULATED WITHOUT SIGNATURES OR WITH FORGED SIGNATURES.

Chiefs of Police, Sheriffs, Marshals and Constables receiving copy of this circular should furnish a copy of the above described stolen currency to banks, bankers, money brokers, gambling houses, pool room keepers and keepers of disorderly houses, and request their co-operation in the arrest of any person or persons presenting any of these bills.

THE UNITED STATES TREASURY DEPARTMENT REFUSES TO REDEEM THESE STOLEN UNSIGNED OR IMPROPERLY SIGNED NOTES.

Officers are warned to have sufficient assistance and be fully armed, when attempting to arrest either of these outlaws, as they are always heavily armed, and will make a determined resistance before submitting to arrest, not hesitating to kill, if necessary.

Foreign ministers and consuls receiving copy of this circular are respectfully requested to give this circular to the police of their city or district.

Postmasters receiving this circular are requested to place same in hands of reliable Police official. Marshal. Constable, Sheriff or Deputy, or a Peace officer.

Below appear the photographs, descriptions and histories of GEORGE PARKER, alias "BUTCH" CASSIDY, alias GEORGE CASSIDY, alias INGERFIELD and HARRY LONGBAUGH alias HARRY ALONZO.

GEORGE PARKER.
First photograph taken July 15, 1894.

432 B

GEORGE PARKER.
Last photograph taken Nov. 21, 1900.

Name..George Parker, alias "Butch" Cassidy, alias George Cassidy, alias Ingerfield.
Nationality....................American
Occupation...............Cowboy; rustler
Criminal Occupation......Bank robber and highwayman, cattle and horse thief
Age..36 yrs. (1901)...*Height*...5 feet 9 in
Weight..165 lbs.....*Build*.......Medium
Complexion..Light..*Color of Hair*.Flaxen
Eyes...Blue......*Mustache*.Sandy, if any
Remarks:—Two cut scars back of head, small scar under left eye, small brown mole calf of leg. "Butch" Cassidy is known as a criminal principally in Wyoming, Utah, Idaho, Colorado and Nevada and has served time in Wyoming State penitentiary at Laramie for grand larceny, but was pardoned January 19th, 1896.

Name.........Harry Longbaugh, alias "Kid" Longbaugh, alias Harry Alonzo alias Frank Jones, alias Frank Boyd, alias the "Sundance Kid"
Nationality.......Swedish-American. *Occupation*...........Cowboy; rustler
Criminal Occupation ....Highwayman, bank burglar, cattle and horse thief
Age ....35 years....................*Height*..............5 feet 10 in
Weight..165 to 175 lbs..............*Build*..........................Good
Eyes ......Blue or gray.............*Complexion* ....Medium
Mustache or Beard.........(if any), natural color brown, reddish tinge
Features....Grecian type........*Nose*..................Rather long
Color of Hair.........Natural color brown, may be dyed; combs it pompadour.

IS BOW-LEGGED AND HIS FEET FAR APART.

Remarks:—Harry Longbaugh served 18 months in jail at Sundance, Cook Co., Wyoming, when a boy, for horse stealing. In December, 1892, Harry Longbaugh, Bill Madden and Henry Bass "held up" a Great Northern train at Malta, Montana. Bass and Madden were tried for this crime, convicted and sentenced to 10 and 14 years respectively; Longbaugh escaped and since has been a fugitive. June 28, 1897, under the name of Frank Jones, Longbaugh participated with Harvey Logan, alias Curry, Tom Day and Walter Putney, in the Belle Fourche, South Dakota, bank robbery. All were arrested, but Longbaugh and Harvey Logan escaped from jail at Deadwood, October 31, the same year. Longbaugh has not since been arrested.

HARRY LONGBAUGH.
Photograph taken Nov. 21, 1900.

We also publish below a photograph, history and description of CAMILLA HANKS, alias O. C. HANKS, alias CHARLEY JONES, alias "DEAF" CHARLEY, who may be found in the company of either PARKER, alias CASSIDY or LONGBAUGH, alias ALONZO, and for whom a proportionate amount of a $5,000.00 Reward is offered by the GREAT NORTHERN EXPRESS COMPANY upon arrest and conviction for participation in the Great Northern (Railway) Express robbery near Wagner, Mont., July 3rd, 1901.

Name..O. C. Hanks, alias Camilla Hanks, alias Charley Jones, alias Deaf Charley
Nationality....American...........*Occupation*...................Cowboy
Criminal Occupation ....Train robber; an ex-convict
Age.......38 years (1901).........*Height*.............5 feet 10 in
Weight..156 lbs...................*Build*......................Good
Complexion...Sandy.............*Color of Hair*..............Auburn
Eyes.......Blue................*Mustache or Beard*......(if any), natural color sandy
Remarks:—Scar from burn, size 25c piece, on right forearm. Small scar right leg, above ankle. Mole near right nipple. Leans his head slightly to the left. Somewhat deaf. Raised at Yorktown, Texas, fugitive from there charged with rape; also wanted in New Mexico on charge of murder. Arrested in Teton County, Montana, 1892, and sentenced to 10 years in the penitentiary at Deer Lodge, for holding up Northern Pacific train near Big Timber, Montana. Released April 30th, 1901.

CAMILLA HANKS.
Photograph taken 1892.

HARVEY LOGAN, alias "KID" CURRY, referred to in our first circular issued from Denver on May 15, 1901, is now under arrest at Knoxville, Tenn., charged with shooting two police officers who were attempting his arrest.

BEN KILPATRICK, alias JOHN ARNOLD, alias "THE TALL TEXAN" of Concho County, Texas, another member of the Harvey Logan band of outlaws, was arrested at St. Louis, Mo., on November 5th, 1901, tried, convicted and sentenced to 15 years at Knoxville, Texas, Sept. 1901, by Sheriff E. S. Briant, while resisting arrest on charge of murder.

WILLIAM CARVER, alias "BILL" CARVER, of Sonora, Sutton County, Texas, another member of this band, was killed at Sonora, Texas, April 1901, by Sheriff E. S. Briant, while resisting arrest on charge of murder.

IN CASE OF AN ARREST immediately notify PINKERTON'S NATIONAL DETECTIVE AGENCY at the nearest of the above listed offices.

Or

JOHN C. FRASER,
Resident Sup't., DENVER, COLO.

Pinkerton's National Detective Agency,
Opera House Block, Denver, Colo.

ABOVE: *The dapper Hole-in-the-Wall Gang, also known as the Wild Bunch. Harry Longbaugh (the Sundance Kid) is seated in the front row, left, George LeRoy Parker (Butch Cassidy) in the front row right.*

TOP LEFT: *Members of the posse mustered by U.S. Marshal Frank A. Hadsell of Wyoming to track down the Wild Bunch.*

LEFT: *Allan Pinkerton's National Detective Agency, with offices in 12 major cities, joined the hunt for the elusive outlaws.*

A cut above most gang leaders was dapper, Utah-born "Butch Cassidy" (George Leroy Parker), who apparently never killed a man during his six-year career in Wyoming Territory. In fact, he boasted that he shot only the horses when pursued by a posse. Twenty-nine-year-old Cassidy formed his gang to rob banks, rustle cattle, and steal mining camp payrolls. In 1899 the group turned to post-office and train robbery with considerable success, escaping to their hideout in the Wyoming mountains, which gave them their nickname, the Hole-in-the-Wall Gang. When the territorial governor asked Washington for help, Attorney General Charles Devens arranged to have Pinkerton detectives aid U.S. Marshal Frank A. Hadsell in pursuing the elusive gang. The Pinkerton Agency circulated mug shots and descriptions of Cassidy and his associate, Harry Longbaugh, alias the Sundance Kid, both identified as "Highwayman, bank robber, cattle and horse thief." But no one succeeded in tracking down the outlaws. The best the pursuers could do was chase them out of Wyoming. In 1901 Cassidy, Longbaugh, and his mistress, Etta Place, took ship for South America, where they continued their criminal career for another decade. Meantime, out West, they had already become legends.

On the Borders and Beyond

In the Southwest, the long border with Mexico presented federal lawmen with a daunting challenge. During the late 1890s the Black Jack gang of New Mexico Territory was a byword for ruthlessness, robbing, and killing during swift raids, then escaping across the border into Mexico. Marshal Edward L. Hall reported to Washington that "they will never be taken alive." In 1896 the gang held up several trains and robbed the post office at Separ, New Mexico. At the time, Deputy Horace W. Loomis had pursued them without success, but several months later Loomis was a passenger on an Arizona and Pacific train when the Black Jack gang tried to hold it up forty miles from Albuquerque. He jumped out into the underbrush with his shotgun and killed gang member Cole Young from ambush, scattering the would-be train robbers. Nevertheless, the next morning they eluded the posse again.

In March 1897 the gang sortied from its Mexican hideout and robbed the Cliff post office and a number of other establishments. Marshal Hall sent out several posses at once to catch the outlaws, who were led by William "Black Jack" Christian. Deputy Fred Higgins paid two informants to lead him to the gang's camp, where a gunfight resulted in Christian's death. But then another outlaw, Tom Ketchum, assumed the name "Black Jack" and led the gang in further depredations in the Arizona Territory, including mail and train robberies, until Marshal W. M. Griffith finally chased the gang back into Mexico. Even so, it would be several more years before the capture or death of most gang members at last put an end to their periodic raids in Arizona and New Mexico. Black Jack Ketchum himself was the first man convicted of train robbery under the New Mexico statute that made it a capital offense: the territory imposed the death sentence.

Animosity between the United States and Mexico made the marshals' job of protecting the border even more difficult after the Civil War, when a flood of new settlers entered Texas, New Mexico, and Arizona. Border raids went in both directions, but the majority involved Mexican soldiers and adventurers crossing the Rio Grande to rob and kill Americans. Federal attorneys and marshals in Texas complained to the Justice Department that their region's peace and

RIGHT: *Train robbers made travel through the frontier West a dangerous enterprise. They caused train wrecks and often killed passengers who resisted.*

ABOVE: *The execution of "Black Jack" Ketchum for train robbery, a capital offense in New Mexico Territory.*

prosperity were constantly disrupted by incursions from Mexico to which the Mexican government turned a blind eye. As a result, when Southwestern settlers made forays across the border into Mexico to rustle, rob, and kill, local juries were reluctant to impose sentence on those whom the marshals brought to justice.

The Cowboys, a gang of American raiders, created constant problems for Virgil Earp when he was deputy marshal of notorious Tombstone, Arizona, during the early 1880s. And Territorial Marshal

Crowley P. Dake got little help from Washington for his beleaguered deputies, especially in the southern part of the territory. Silver mining had made Tombstone a boom town, and disappointed prospectors often turned to drink and crime in the feverish atmosphere engendered by the get-rich-quick mentality. The Cowboys gang had made frequent raids into and out of Sonora, Mexico, rustling cattle, robbing Wells Fargo stages, and shooting to kill when they were pursued. In 1878 they had shot down two of Dake's deputy marshals, J. H. Adams and Cornelius Finley, and, under pressure from Attorney General Wayne MacVeagh to stop the raiders, Dake had commissioned Virgil Earp as deputy marshal for Tombstone in November 1879. Unfortunately, Virgil also accepted a dual commission as town marshal of Tombstone, and the lucrative business of collecting taxes and licensing fees from merchants and prostitutes soon took precedence in his mind over other aspects of law enforcement.

The marshal's three brothers, Wyatt, Morgan, and James, shared Virgil's free-wheeling style and his eagerness to make money. James opened a saloon, Wyatt went into gambling and schemed for the job of Cochise County sheriff, and Morgan rode shotgun for Wells Fargo between Tucson and Tombstone, while also working part time as a town policeman. With all this going on in Tombstone, the Earp brothers were reluctant to chase the Cowboys gang for any great distance along the Mexican border, despite the constant urgings of Marshal Dake in Prescott.

In June 1881 Mexican soldiers killed Cowboy leader Newman H. (Old Man) Clanton during a raid. His sons, Ike and Billy, were almost certainly part of his gang, but they were better known in Tombstone as visiting cattlemen (who sometimes had stock with altered brands for sale). When Ike and Billy took part in the famous gunfight with the Earps at the O.K. Corral on October 26, Marshal Dake assumed that Virgil had taken on the Clantons to stop the Cowboy raids. In fact, the legendary shootout had nothing to do with Virgil's role as a deputy marshal. It resulted from a feud between Wyatt and Ike Clanton, inflamed by Wyatt's hard-drinking dentist friend John (Doc) Holliday, an acquaintance from Dodge City days. The combustible mix of the ruthless Clanton brothers, with their friends Frank and Tom McLaury, and the excitable Earp trio (James was not involved) finally detonated one day when Cochise County sheriff John Behan tried to disarm Billy Clanton and Frank McLaury. Insults and blows had already passed between the Clanton group and the Earps, who were on their way down the street toward the corral. Ike and Billy refused to give up their guns unless the Earps did. Behan pleaded with the Earps not to get involved any further, but they pushed him out of the way and advanced down Fremont Street. With them was Holliday, whom they had deputized on the spot. A minute later the shooting started.

Territory
~~State~~ of Arizona
COUNTY OF ~~Yavapai~~
Pima

I, W. W. Earp do solemnly
swear that I will support the Constitution of the United States and the laws of this
Territory; that I will true faith and allegiance bear to the same, and defend them
against all enemies whatsoever; and that I will faithfully and impartially discharge
the duties of the office of Deputy United States Marshal
according to the best of my abilities, so help God.

W W Earp

Sworn and subscribed to before me this
day of November A.D. 187

U.S. Dist. Clerk

BELOW: *Reckless John (Doc) Holliday became friendly with Wyatt Earp in the wide-open cattle town of Dodge City, Kansas.*

TOP LEFT: *Wyatt Earp abused his position as a U.S. deputy marshal to take vengeance on members of the Cowboys gang for the ambush of his brother Virgil.*

ABOVE: *The famous O.K. Corral in Tombstone, Arizona, scene of the shootout between the Earps and the Clantons.*

LEFT: *The warrant signed by Virgil Earp when he accepted the office of deputy marshal for the Southern District of Arizona in 1879.*

OVERLEAF: *The Earps and Doc Holliday romanticized into folk heroes in the film* Gunfight at the O.K. Corral.

When it was over, Billy Clanton and both the McLaurys were dead, three men were wounded, and two were unharmed – Ike Clanton and Wyatt Earp.

This kind of "law enforcement" was too much even for rough-and-ready Tombstone. Friends of the three victims charged that they had been murdered in the streets. Virgil was suspended as town marshal, and Sheriff Behan charged Wyatt and Holliday with murder. Protracted hearings before the local magistrate resulted in the release of both prisoners, with reprimands, but public confidence in the Earps as peacekeepers was shaken badly. A few months later, when Virgil recovered from the leg wound he had received in the shootout, he was ambushed and shot in the arm. Wyatt prevailed upon Marshal Dake to commission him as a U.S. deputy marshal – ostensibly to hunt down additional members of the Cowboys gang. In fact, he used his position, and a $3,000 advance from the Justice Department, to go on a rampage against Virgil's assailants. In the end, the U.S. Army had to help the marshals restore order in the battle-scarred region between Tombstone and the Mexican border.

10209-116

ABOVE: *The legendary lawman of the West on his way to a showdown, as portrayed by Gary Cooper in* High Noon.

LEFT: *Another idealized look at the role of the U.S. marshal: television's "Gunsmoke" series of the 1960s, which even gave rise to a board game.*

ABOVE: *Clint Eastwood as the steely-eyed marshal in* Hang 'Em High.

LEFT: *John Wayne (left) and Robert Mitchum contributed to the myth of the Western lawman in epics like* El Dorado.

The young man who replaced Virgil Earp as town marshal of Tombstone was named David Neagle. Unlike the flamboyant Earp, however, Neagle was altogether serious about trying to define both the rights and the duties that pertained to his office. And this was just as well, for he would soon be involved in a case that would go a long way toward clarifying just how far a marshal's powers went.

By 1889 Neagle had been made a U.S. deputy marshal and had been charged with guarding Supreme Court Justice Stephen Field from threats to his life resulting from one of his earlier judicial decisions. These threats eventually materialized in the dining room of the Lathrop, California, train station on the morning of August 14 in the marshals' centennial year of 1889. Neagle and Field were having breakfast when six-foot David Terry approached the justice from behind and struck him on the head. Neagle leaped between Justice Field and his assailant and ordered Terry to back away, declaring, "I am an officer."

Terry recognized the deputy marshal, whom he had slashed at with his Bowie knife in a brawl a year before. With a growl of rage he reached under his vest, as if to pull the knife, and Neagle shot him through the heart, believing, as he said later, that "it was life or death with me." Pandemonium reigned in the dining roon as Neagle escorted the injured Justice Field back to the Pullman car on which they were traveling to San Francisco. On the platform, Sarah Terry, David Terry's wife, urged frightened onlookers to seize the man who had killed her husband. In due course, Constable Walker of Lathrop township boarded the train and arrested Neagle.

Justice Field urged the young deputy not to go with the constable, arguing that the shooting had been done in the line of duty under his mandate from the federal government. But Neagle insisted on showing respect for a local officer of the law by submitting to the arrest. He was then taken to the San Joaquin County jail and booked on a charge of murder: it had not helped his case that no knife had been found on Terry's body.

Matters could have gone very ill for David Neagle, because at this time U.S. marshals were liable for any action taken in the line of duty that was not covered by a specific federal law or court order. A marshal arrested by state authorities could count on little besides free legal advice from the executive branch of the government. Nevertheless, in this instance the Ninth Circuit Court – Justice Field abstaining – ordered Neagle released. Sheriff Thomas Cunningham of San Joaquin Country promptly appealed the case to the United States Supreme Court.

On March 4 and 5, 1890, the Supreme Court heard oral arguments from Attorney General Miller, who had ordered Neagle to protect Field, and from California attorney general G. A. Johnson, who wanted the deputy marshal tried for murder within his jurisdiction. In a precedent-setting decision, the Court ruled on

FAR LEFT: *A deputy marshal's badge of the 1890s, when westward expansion was almost complete.*

LEFT: *The Dodge City, Kansas, Peace Commission of 1882 included William Barclay (Bat) Masterson (back row, right) and Wyatt Earp (front row, second from left).*

BELOW: *Texas trail drivers delivered 250,000 head of cattle a year to the Dodge City railhead for shipment east in the late 1870s.*

ABOVE: *Deputy Marshal Bud Ledbetter was widely respected in the Twin Territories formed from Oklahoma and Indian Territory.*

ABOVE: *Bat Masterson's checkered career included stints as an Indian fighter, peace officer, gambler, and journalist.*

LEFT: *Deputy Marshal Steve Burke combined his role as a lawman with a career as a preacher.*

April 14 in Neagle's favor, with Justice Field again abstaining. In essence, the Court held that Neagle, as a U.S. marshal, had in fact been duty-bound to protect Field from "murderous attack," that this duty derived both from the larger context of U.S. law and from Congress's original intent in creating the office of U.S. marshal, and that the absence of a specific law or court order authorizing Neagle's action in no way diminished that duty. This decision vastly enlarged the powers of all U.S. marshals.

Historically, the United States border with Canada had been more peaceful than the nation's southern boudary with Mexico, but in 1866 it became the scene of an improbable assault that required the intervention of marshals from both northern New York and Washington, D.C. An Irish-immigrant group called the Fenians launched an attack on British Canada from Buffalo, New York. The Fenians had left their homeland, but not their patriotism, behind during the potato famine, and they had close ties with the Fenian Society in Ireland. Both groups were committed to freeing Ireland from British domination.

It is still unclear how the conquest of Canada figured in Fenian plans – whether the world's largest country was to be taken hostage or used as a launching pad for the invasion of the British Isles. But after the Civil War recruits flocked to the Fenian standard, and Irish Americans gave generously to the cause. The group took its name from the ancient Irish Army, *Fianna Eirann*, that sought to repel foreign invaders who had taken over their land.

In 1865 a Fenian convention held in Cincinnati voted to carry out the invasion of Canada. Led by General John O'Neill, some 600 men converged on Buffalo in the spring of 1866 to cross the Niagara River and capture Fort Erie. The city greeted the Fenians enthusiastically, and a large number of weapons was shipped to the scene. Secretary of State William H. Seward warned Attorney General James Speed about this threat to the neutrality laws, and Speed sent U.S. Marshal Edward Dodd to Buffalo to prevent the Fenian raid. With him was U.S. Attorney William A. Dart. Before they could take decisive action, however, the Fenians had crossed the river in canal boats and landed at Waterloo.

O'Neill's force had the advantage of surprise over the Canadian militia at Ridgeway, where they clashed the next day, June 2, but the Fenians' further progress was frustrated by the marshals, who had already blocked off both their resupply of weapons and their reinforcements. Dart was eager to prosecute O'Neill and his followers, but as the summer wore on it became clear that public sympathy in Erie County would preclude their conviction. In the interim, Henry Stanbery succeeded James Speed as attorney general, and he agreed with Dart that it would be better to release the Fenians than to have them tried and acquitted. O'Neill and his followers promptly began planning another invasion of Canada.

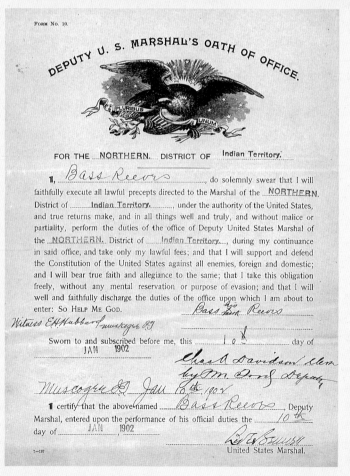

LEFT: *Choctaw Indian Amos Maytubby (left) served as a deputy marshal with (from left) Zek Miller, Neely Factor, and Bob L. Fortune.*

BOTTOM LEFT: *Black deputy marshal Bass Reeves took the oath of office for the Northern District of Indian Territory in 1902.*

BOTTOM CENTER: *Deputy Reeves rose to the position of U.S. marshal for Indian Territory, based at Fort Smith, Arkansas.*

BELOW: *Reeves and his mount prepare to go "on the scout" in Indian Territory with fellow deputies.*

Marshals in northern New York followed up on occasional reports of Fenian activity for several years, but in the event, it was Vermont that O'Neill chose as the jumping-off point for his next incursion, in May 1870. The border towns of St. Albans and Malone bustled with the new Irish army, and Marshal George P. Foster was sent to enforce the neutrality laws. With him was Deputy Thomas Failey and a small posse of Vermont citizens.

When the marshals entered O'Neill's camp it was clear that they would be taken prisoner before they could make any arrests: the Fenians were well armed and adamant about crossing into Canada, where forces were already gathering to repel them. Thus Marshal Foster and Deputy Failey could do no more than withdraw to a nearby house as O'Neill's forces engaged the Canadians. Again the Fenians could make no headway against the defenders, and when O'Neill rushed back into Vermont to bring up reinforcements, the marshals emerged from behind the house and arrested him. At that point the invasion fell apart, with several more Fenian officers placed under arrest along with their leader.

General O'Neill was finally sentenced to two years in jail, but he was promptly pardoned by President Ulysses S. Grant, as were his officers – sympathy for the Fenians was not confined to Erie County. But even O'Neill was too discouraged to attempt another invasion of Canada, although the Fenians remained active – and vocal – about their cause for years.

As the United States became a growing power in world affairs, it followed Europe's example in protecting its nationals in the Far East by treaties that enshrined the principle of extraterritoriality. China, Japan, Siam, and other non-Christian countries had been obliged to waive the right to try American traders, travelers, or residents in local courts according to local laws, and Americans in Far Eastern countries thus obeyed only their own national laws, with civil and criminal disputes heard in their own courts.

A system of consular courts was created by legislation enacted in June 1860 covering eight Far Eastern countries: Japan, Siam, China (which had four courts), Persia, Tripoli, Tunis, Morocco, and Muscat. At the same time, Congress created the office of U.S. marshal to the consular courts and authorized the president to appoint seven marshals to these positions – one each for Japan, Siam, and Turkey, which had observed extraterritoriality with the United States since 1830, and four for China.

The consular marshals, unlike their counterparts in the United States, enjoyed a modest salary in addition to the fees they received for specific services. Their duties were almost identical: serving processes, making arrests, keeping prisoners in custody, and executing the orders of the courts. The system was widely resented by the host countries, implying as it did a contempt for the

ABOVE: *Chinese resentment of extraterritoriality exploded in the Boxer Rebellion of 1900.*

TOP LEFT: *The badge of the consular court in China, 1860–1943.*

CENTER LEFT: *Deputy marshal's badge for the Territory of China.*

LEFT: *The Fenian invasion of Canada, May 1866.*

sovereignty of the nations involved, but it persisted for decades. China's Boxer Rebellion of 1900 was an outburst of violence against extraterritoriality imposed by the Western nations. Other Asian countries were more covert in their resentment.

In 1907 all the consular courts except those in China were transformed into a single U.S. district court with four divisions. Federal judges and attorneys took over the role of consular officials, and the consular marshals worked for the district court. Only in China did the system persist until 1943. The consular courts were the measure of the federal government's resolve to exercise total control over the nation's foreign policy.

Industrialization, World War, and Social Change

By 1890 westward expansion had almost reached its limits, and Americans were deeply involved in the profound social changes attendant upon industrialization. Labor was organizing rapidly, in spite of resistance from management, and was vigorously demanding a more equitable share in the new industrial economy. In most major American industries, trusts and monopolies were ascendant and virtually unregulated in their employment policies, yet the federal government persistently threw its weight behind management rather than labor: strikes were seen as a threat to society, and U.S. marshals were thus often thrust into the role of strike-breakers. "Contempt of court" was the commonest charge

BOTTOM LEFT: *Labor leader and socialist Eugene Debs, founder of the American Railway Union.*

RIGHT: *Wyoming's Marshal Frank A. Hadsell saw his territory become a state in 1890, when its population was still only 60,000. Here, Hadsell's counter-signature on the oath sworn by Harry R. Logue when he was deputized.*

BELOW: *Deputy marshals oversee the start-up of a freight train in East St. Louis, Illinois, during the Great Railway Strike of 1886.*

FORM NO. 10.

Original

DEPUTY U. S. MARSHAL'S OATH OF OFFICE.

FOR THE ----- DISTRICT OF WYOMING.

I, HARRY R. LOGUE, do solemnly swear that I will faithfully execute all lawful precepts directed to the Marshal of the ----- District of Wyoming, under the authority of the United States, and true returns make, and in all things well and truly, and without malice or partiality, perform the duties of the office of Deputy United States Marshal of the ----- District of Wyoming, during my continuance in said office, and take only my lawful fees; and that I will support and defend the Constitution of the United States against all enemies, foreign and domestic; and I will bear true faith and allegiance to the same; that I take this obligation freely, without any mental reservation or purpose of evasion; and that I will well and faithfully discharge the duties of the office upon which I am about to enter: SO HELP ME GOD.

Harry R Logue

Sworn to and subscribed before me, this 11th day of July, 1906. My Commission. Expires Feb 21. 1910. Cheyenne, Wyo., JUL 17 1906

Porter B Coolidge
Notary Public

I certify that the above-named Harry R. Logue, Deputy Marshal, entered upon the performance of his official duties the sixteenth day of July, 1906.

Frank A Hadsell
United States Marshal.

against laborers who went on strike, and the Justice Department was quick to use it.

Eugene Debs founded the American Railway Union in 1893, and by the following year it had 150,000 members. At that time the economy was in a serious depression, compounded by multiple bank and business failures. By 1894 millions were out of work, and struggling businesses increasingly slashed the wages of workers, most of whom were unable to sustain the cuts. One disastrous result was the celebrated Pullman Strike, the first in a series of struggles that would last for decades.

It began in May 1894, in Pullman, Illinois, south of Chicago – a company town for the Pullman Palace Car Company. Longstanding resentments against Pullman, along with a series of wage cuts, precipitated the strike on May 11. When the company locked the strikers out, they appealed for help at the June convention of the

American Railway Union. The A.R.U. voted to boycott Pullman cars by refusing to move them, and Debs agreed that if any member of the union was fired as a result, the other members would go on strike against the offending railroad. The railroad managers of course sided with Pullman, hoping to break the A.R.U.

Some 18,000 union workers went on strike late in June, and rail transport in the Midwest and the West was paralyzed. Because transport of the U.S. mail was affected, U.S. Attorney General Richard Olney had the excuse he wanted, and an omnibus injunction was drawn up whereby strikers were identified as disrupting interstate commerce and the carriage of the mail: strikers were forbidden to approach the railyards or to encourage railroad employees to leave their jobs. Deputy marshals served the injunction on Debs and other A.R.U. officials on July 2, as Illinois Marshal John Arnold swore in the last of 600 extra deputies whom Olney had authorized him to hire when advised that the situation in Chicago was desperate. Ultimately, 5,000 such deputies would be sworn in, of whom more than two-thirds would secretly be in the pay of the railroads.

Predictably, the strikers sneered at Marshal Arnold's reading of the injunction on July 2 and overturned three boxcars on the tracks. Arnold wired Washington for military assistance from nearby Fort Sheridan, and two thousand soldiers were dispatched. A pitched battle ensued, with troops and deputies fighting the strikers for days, amid vandalism, arson, and total disruption of railway service. On July 7 strikers attacked state militiamen sent in by Governor John Altgeld. Four strikers were killed and 20 wounded. Although other areas affected by the strike did not experience the same level of violence, U.S. marshals throughout the Midwest and the West were called upon to enforce the omnibus injunctions protecting the mail trains, in some cases with the assistance of troops, as in Chicago.

On July 10 Debs and others in the A.R.U. were indicted for conspiracy to disrupt the mails and conspiracy to commit violence. On January 8, 1985, Debs was sentenced to six months in prison for contempt of court in defying the omnibus injunction. Other union officials were sentenced to three months. It was a staggering defeat for organized labor, the more so since the federal government would thereafter continue to deny the unions' right to exist until Woodrow Wilson took office in 1913.

RIGHT: *The army was called in to help break the Pullman Strike of 1894, in which four strikers were killed and the burgeoning labor movement was almost stifled.*

ABOVE: *German aliens suspected of being dangerous to national security are arrested in New York City and consigned to police vans in 1917.*

LEFT: *The marshals posted notices that warned German residents against trespassing into military installations, war-industry facilities, ports, and other sensitive areas.*

Early in Wilson's second administration, on April 6, 1917, the United States entered World War I by declaring war on Germany. The Alien Act of 1798 was the guideline for the internment or regulation of Germans resident in the United States. Attorney General Thomas W. Gregory advised U.S. attorneys and marshals nationwide of the regulations they were to enforce in registering and monitoring the activities of all German males in the United States. Those whom federal officials suspected of being "dangerous to the peace and safety" of the nation were arrested and interned in prison camps at Fort Oglethorpe and Fort McPherson, Georgia. By the end of June the marshals had arrested almost 300 enemy aliens, and another 600 had been interned by the end of the year. Before the war ended, more than 6,000 Germans would be arrested under presidential warrant.

Registered enemy aliens who were not interned were subject to strict regulations. They were forbidden to own radios, ciphers, or weapons, or to approach within half a mile of any military installation, ship, or factory engaged in the production of war matériel. Marshals were also involved in enforcing measures aimed at public opposition to the war, the main justification for this being the Espionage and Sedition Acts of 1917, which set limits on the right of free speech. They were also charged with arresting violaters of the Selective Service laws and those who opposed it. The turmoil wrought by the massive changes of the previous four decades was

RIGHT: *A federal agent padlocks a Detroit business for violation of the Volstead Act during the Prohibition era.*

LEFT: *A cell constructed for detention of enemy aliens in a federal building during World War I.*

BELOW: *An internment camp for aliens at Fort Douglas, Utah.*

reflected in the struggle to find a new balance between governmental power and individual rights, many of the latter being considerably damaged in the process.

Passage of the Volstead Act on October 27, 1919, ushered in the Prohibition era, which lasted from 1920 until 1933. The newly created office of commissioner of Prohibition, as well as the agents for enforcing the law against the sale of intoxicating beverages, were placed under the commissioner of Internal Revenue in the Treasury Department. But it was the marshals, under the Department of Justice, who made the arrests resulting from the investigations, and as the number of investigations and arrests rapidly spiraled, the marshals found themselves saddled with an enormous workload. In addition, the marshals were responsible for seizing breweries and distilleries and all vehicles and equipment used by bootleggers. Guards then had to be hired to protect seized properties, and everything had to be inventoried and eventually disposed of.

LEFT: *Al Capone prepares to leave Chicago for the federal penitentiary in Atlanta after his sentencing for income-tax evasion in 1931.*

Trials of major racketeers such as Al Capone, who left Illinois for Florida after warrants for his arrest on charges of income tax evasion were issued in 1931, created special problems for the marshals. Two deputies had to chase the mobster to Florida to effect the arrest, while the Chicago office struggled to issue subpoenas to the many witnesses involved in the case that had been put together by the Internal Revenue Service. As always, the Justice Department was tight-fisted when it came to paying the extra expenses resulting from the extra work.

TOP RIGHT: *Capone passes the time playing cards on the train trip from Chicago to Atlanta in the custody of Deputy Marshal Henry Laubenheimer.*

RIGHT: *U.S. deputy marshals and IRS agents search the Cotton Club in Cicero, Illinois, for Capone's records.*

ABOVE: *Distillery equipment confiscated in a 1920s raid by federal agents is turned over to the marshals for safekeeping.*

LEFT: *Lola Anderson Young of the District of Columbia was commissioned as a deputy marshal in 1919.*

As Prohibition proved inreasingly difficult to enforce, the federal government began to rely ever more upon state and local authorities (who were equally unsuccessful) and to increase the number of specialized agencies for law enforcement in other areas, such as kidnapping to bank fraud. By the time Prohibition was repealed in 1933 the new breed of federal lawmen had come into increasing prominence, and of all the new agencies, the Federal Bureau of Investigation, headed by J. Edgar Hoover, had attracted the most attention and admiration from the general public.

As the specialist agencies evolved, the U.S. marshals found themselves at a growing disadvantage in terms of professionalism. Their role within the Justice Department was beginning to dwindle to that of court policemen and process servers. To be sure, in 1937 they had finally been granted a minimum salary, rather than fees alone, but that salary was only $1,800.

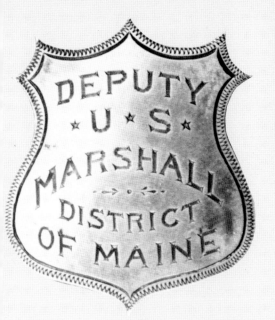

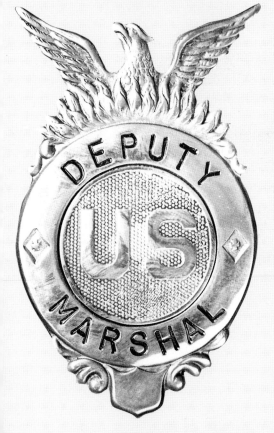

U.S. DEPARTMENT OF JUSTICE

UNITED STATES MARSHALS

BULLETIN

TABLE OF CONTENTS

1. Purchase of cars
2. Marshal Manual
3. Public Relations
4. Tort Claims
5. Escapes
6. Advance Deposits
   Bankruptcy
7. Marshals Conference
8. Post Office Boxes
9. Alien Enemy Property
10. Relatives as Guards
11. Travel Regulations
12. Driver Responsibility
13. Air Mail
14. New Marshals

No. 1   November 1, 1946

LEFT: *An assortment of silver star and circle badges: early 1900s.*

ABOVE AND TOP: *A shield-shaped badge from the District of Maine and a circle badge with eagle.*

TOP RIGHT: *The first* United States Marshals Bulletin *was issued by the Justice Department in 1946.*

In an effort to attract younger candidates, rather than the many retired policemen and soldiers who had been filling the ranks of deputy marshals, the Justice Department imposed new regulations in 1939. Attorney General Frank Murphy required that deputies be from 23 to 50 years old, have a high school education or its equivalent, be physically fit, and, preferably, have some experience in law enforcement. Within these guidelines, the marshals were still allowed to recruit their deputies directly, and new regulations extended job protection to the deputies beyond the term of the marshal who had hired them. This made it possible to consider the office of deputy marshal as a career, which had never been the case before. In 1946 the Justice Department issued the first *United States Marshals Bulletin* to every district, which promised that a manual for the office and a handbook for deputies were being prepared. But it would be another decade before the marshals were ready to resume their rightful place in federal law enforcement.

New Roles and Responsibilities

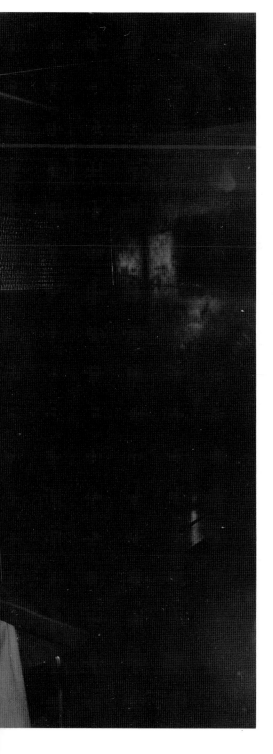

U.S. marshals would be deeply involved in the trauma and turmoil of the 1960s and the decades that followed, and the nature of that involvement would do much to refurbish the marshals' somewhat diminished reputation. The process began in the early days of the black civil rights movement.

When the Supreme Court ordered the states to desegregate their schools "with all deliberate speed" in 1954, what role the U.S. marshals would play in implementing the Court's decision was far from clear. They lacked leadership, centralization, and representation at the Department of Justice. As always, their financial footing was insecure, and they were at the mercy of politicians in power at both the local and national levels. They still worked largely alone within their judicial districts, to which their authority was limited, and there was little coordination between the districts or sharing of their meager resources.

In 1956 the Justice Department addressed these problems by recommending the creation of an Executive Office for U.S. Marshals. Attorney General Herbert Brownell, Jr., approved the proposal, and it went into effect on December 17, 1956. The new office was to be supervised by the deputy attorney general. Its mandate was to provide general direction, supervision, and executive assistance to the marshals; to monitor their performance; and to facilitate the exchange of ideas and information among them. Clive W. Palmer, the deputy attorney general's executive assistant, was put in charge of a small staff of professionals and support people – 17 in all. Nine of them were field examiners who reported their audits of the various judicial districts to Washington.

Promising as all this was, it took time for it to have much impact on day-to-day operations. At first it was mostly a matter of paperwork: new forms and rules for filling them out proliferated, but the marshals still remained largely isolated in the performance of their duties. But at least they now had a voice within the Justice Department and an organizational framework that would, with time, grow larger and stronger.

When President Dwight D. Eisenhower appointed Carlton G. Beall U.S. marshal for the District of Columbia in 1954, the marshals' image began to change. After a long period of being regarded primarily as bailiffs and outdated holdovers from frontier days, the deputy marshals began to be perceived as efficient, take-charge young law-enforcement officers. This was due in part to Beall's personality and to his background as the sheriff of Prince Georges County, Maryland, where he began to recruit deputy marshals for the District of Columbia. Such men as Al Butler, Ellis Duley, Don

RIGHT: *A watchman's badge from the marshal's national office in Washington, D.C.*

RIGHT: *The bailiff's badge, worn in the courtroom, where marshals have maintained order throughout their history.*

LEFT: *Transporting prisoners from a federal courthouse to a place of detention.*

Forsht, Bob Haislip, and Frank Vandegrift brought with them to Washington reputations for energy and innovation, along with a thirst for adventure.

To maintain the *esprit* of his new deputies – all of them in their early to mid-thirties – Beall had to give them something to do besides serving warrants. Since the District of Columbia marshals also acted as the district's sheriff, the new deputies were first set to work making arrests and pursuing fugitives. Then the Bureau of Prisons was persuaded to organize a training class for deputy marshals that was attended by Butler, Forsht, and Duley. Subsequently, the bureau recommended to Clive Palmer that the three young men take charge of training deputies all over the

country. Under the supervision of attorney John Palmer, who had recently joined the Executive Office, Butler, Forsht, and Duley held seminars to train deputy marshals from all over the country during the next few years. Professionalism was increasing, and pride was increasing along with it.

New leadership for the marshals emerged in the form of James J. P. McShane, a former New York City homocide detective and Golden Gloves Boxer. McShane had become friendly with Robert F. Kennedy in the late 1950s, and the future attorney general had persuaded him to come to Washington, first as a member of the Senate racketeering committee staff, then as his personal bodyguard during John F. Kennedy's presidential campaign of 1960. McShane served as chief of security for the campaign, and when the Kennedys took office he was appointed U.S. marshal for the District of Columbia.

In Washington, McShane, who would be known as Uncle Jim by his deputies, worked closely with Butler, Forsht, Duley, and others who took their role as law-enforcement agents seriously. They saw in him both a natural leader and a man who had immediate access to the sources of power in the Kennedy administration. And the

ABOVE: *James Meredith (third from left) leaves the University of Mississippi campus at Oxford with federal marshals after being refused admission by the state's governor, Ross Barnett, on September 20, 1962.*

TOP RIGHT: *U.S. Marshal James McShane (left) serves the Mississippi lieutenant governor, Paul Johnson, (right) with papers ordering the admission of James Meredith to the university six days after he was turned away.*

RIGHT: *It took both the marshals and the army to enroll Meredith at the University of Mississippi on September 30, 1962.*

LEFT: *Marshals escort black children from a newly integrated New Orleans school in the autumn of 1960.*

ABOVE: *Black and white Freedom Marchers cross the Alabama River on March 10, 1965, to encounter state troops at Selma who turned them back.*

Kennedys saw in him just the man to head the struggle for enforcement of the court-ordered desegregation of Southern schools. When Clive Palmer resigned as head of the Executive Office for U.S. Marshals in May 1962, McShane was appointed to his position and took up the new title of chief U.S. marshal.

As the FBI and the army were also doing, McShane met Southern resistance to the new laws head-to-head. In September 1962 he confronted Mississippi Lieutenant Governor Paul Johnson at the University of Mississippi over the court-ordered registration of James Meredith at the all-white school. McShane led his deputy marshals onto the Oxford campus and escorted Meredith to the registrar's office, where he was duly enrolled, despite violent protest – so violent, indeed, that by September 30 President Kennedy had to order military forces to Oxford to quell a major riot. Yet despite all the hostility, until Meredith's graduation the following August, marshals remained steadfastly on the campus to protect him.

Racial tensions were not confined to the South. In July 1964 they erupted in New York City's Harlem and other urban black ghettos and spread rapidly to Brooklyn's Bedford-Stuyvesant section, several New Jersey cities, Chicago, and Philadelphia. In all such cases U.S. marshals worked closely with local police, national guardsmen, and other forces whenever federal laws were violated or government property was threatened. It was only in the South that the state and local law-enforcement officers actively resisted the thrust of the civil rights movement.

When the Reverend Martin Luther King, Jr., and 4,000 blacks attempted to march from Selma to Montgomery, Alabama, in the spring of 1965, they were attacked by Alabama state troopers for their protest of the state's refusal to register black voters. One demonstrater died as a result of the police attack with clubs and tear gas. King called off a second attempt to make the 54-mile walk when additional violence was threatened by the troopers. At that point President Lyndon B. Johnson sent a hundred deputy marshals to Selma to safeguard the marchers. A hundred FBI agents accompanied them to assess the risks involved, and almost 4,000 soldiers protected the route. In cities like Little Rock, New Orleans, and Tuscaloosa, Alabama, deputy marshals were on hand to enforce court-ordered desegregation and protect the Freedom Riders, activists, and black schoolchildren whose lives were at risk.

As the 1960s wore on, there was growing public dissatisfaction with the war in Vietnam, and U.S. marshals were called upon to protect government buildings from antiwar demonstrators. On October 21, 1967, some 35,000 protesters converged on Washington to demonstrate at the Defense Department. More than 600 of them were arrested while trying to enter the Pentagon. Once again, the marshals had blocked the path. To be sure, they had been backed by regular Army troops, but only when the civilian power of the government, represented by the marshals, was overcome could the Army provide emergency support, and it fell to the marshals to make the arrests — a civilian power not usually invested in the military. As so often before in their history, the U.S. marshals had been obliged to stand between a rock and a hard place.

PREVIOUS PAGES: *Deputy marshals protect the First Baptist Church in Montgomery, Alabama, from a hostile mob during an address by the Reverend Martin Luther King, Jr. (inset) in 1961.*

RIGHT: *Troops in riot formation line up before the Mall entrance to the Pentagon during the anti-Vietnam War demonstration of October 21, 1967.*

LEFT: *Helmeted marshals subdue an antiwar demonstrator at the Pentagon as the peaceful protest turns violent.*

RIGHT: *Shield-shaped deputy marshal's badge with eagle, pre-1960.*

In 1969 the marshals took a giant step toward collective autonomy when the Executive Office for U.S. Marshals was transformed into the U.S. Marshals Service, with control of the district budgets and the hiring of deputies. For the first time, marshals all over the country, and in U.S. territories and possessions, could count on specific guidance from the executive branch of the government. They had a headquarters. They had a bureaucracy to communicate with other government bureaucracies on their behalf. They had a new emphasis on training, regulation, and accountability. Now the only question was whether their tradition of independence and district autonomy could be successfully wed to the demands of centralization, new technology, and broader responsibilities. The thrust toward that balance has characterized the history of the Marshals Service to the early 1990s.

ABOVE: *The second national badge, issued in 1969.*

TOP RIGHT: *A distinctive badge cut from a Mexican five-peso coin.*

FAR RIGHT: *Emblem of a chief deputy marshal.*

RIGHT: *The classic five-pointed, ball-tipped star.*

The presidential campaign of Richard M. Nixon had "law and order" as one of its major planks. And it was the Nixon administration, beginning in 1969, that expanded the scope of the marshals' role. Under Attorney General John Mitchell and his successors, the marshals undertook or expanded programs in court, personal, and witness security; control of air piracy and civil disturbances; internal inspections; and prisoner transportation. With a headquarters, specialization could become a factor as never before. Experts in court security or fugitive investigations joined the headquarters staff and imparted their expertise to marshals in the field. Professional standards were codified, and these standards were applied to the recruitment and training process to ensure that suitable men and women entered the service. By 1974 the central organization had assumed the form it bears today.

The Director of the U.S. Marshals Service is now appointed by the president and directs nationwide operations from the impressive headquarters building in Arlington, Virginia, which was completed in 1988. There are 95 district offices, each headed by a presidentially-appointed U.S. marshal, and personnel stationed at more than 350 locations throughout the 50 states and from Guam to Puerto Rico and the Virgin Islands. Some 3,000 deputy U.S. marshals and career employees perform the day-to-day missions of the service, which occupies a uniquely central position in the federal justice system.

ABOVE: *Marshals work closely with agents of the Drug Enforcement Administration to seize properties being used as drug havens.*

LEFT: *Deputy marshals get weapons training at the Federal Law Enforcement Training Center in Glynco, Georgia.*

Today virtually every federal law-enforcement initiative involves the Marshals Service: the custody, care, and transportation of federal offenders; tracking and apprehension of federal criminals who jump bail, violate parole, or escape from prison; protection of the courts, judges, attorneys, and witnesses; enforcement of court orders; and management of assets seized or forfeited as a result of their having been acquired from the profits of designated criminal activities, including drug trafficking and organized crime.

Deputy U.S. marshals form the permanent corps of the service's sworn law-enforcement officers, a corps made up of men and women from every ethnic group. Generally, they are college graduates. Many come to the service from careers in local law enforcement or other fields, including teaching, sales, business, and technology.

Recruits receive a total of 14 weeks of intensive training at the Federal Law Enforcement Training Center in Glynco, Georgia. The

first 8 weeks are devoted to such areas as general law enforcement, criminal investigations, and forensics. The other 6 weeks are spent in the U.S. Marshals Service Training Academy, where recruits learn the more specific aspects of the work of deputy marshals. After initial training, recruits return to Glynco frequently for in-service training sessions.

Since 1971 the Marshals Service has had a Special Operations Group (SOG), which receives intensive training at its own Training Center at Camp Beauregard, Louisiana. SOG deputy marshals respond to high-threat and emergency situations, including major civil disorders, terrorist incidents, and hostage situations involving federal law or property violations. The Special Operations umbrella also covers the Air Operations Branch and the Missile Escort Program, which provides security to the Defense Department and the U.S. Air Force during the movement of Minuteman and Cruise missiles between military facilities. The Air Operations Branch, centered in Oklahoma City, operates aircraft used for prisoner transportation and other service missions. It flies SOG teams and other personnel to the sites of emergency situations, carries out international prisoner movements, and conducts prisoner exchanges between the United States and other countries.

As the Marshals Service has expanded, so, too, has the role that women have played in it: there are now over 200 women deputy marshals, a fourfold increase over the number employed as recently as 1975. To be sure, female marshals are hardly a recent innovation. Although existing official records are too scanty to permit us to know precisely when the first woman marshal was deputized, it was probably sometime in the second half of the nineteenth century. We know, for example, from an old issue of *The Illustrated Police News* that U.S. Deputy Marshal Ada Carnutt single-handedly arrested two wanted perjurers in Indian Territory in 1893, and we have no reason to suppose that she was the first such federal lawwoman. Certainly women marshals were serving in China during the Boxer Rebellion at the turn of the century, and by the 1930s women marshals were being appointed directly by U.S. federal courts. The first presidentially-appointed woman marshal, Faith P. Evans of Hawaii, was deputized by Ronald Reagan in 1982. Today, women serve in every branch of the Marshals Service, including the high-risk SOG, and have played important parts in many of the service's most celebrated recent cases.

LEFT: *Members of the Special Operations Group train for riot control with masks to protect them from tear gas.*

One facet of the modern Marshals Service's activities that has drawn a good deal of public attention concerns the protection of witnesses. Masks, hoods, and other devices are used to conceal the identity of government witnesses against major organized-crime figures and other defendants when they testify in court or before Congressional hearings under the protection of the Witness Security Program. This new responsibility fell to the Marshals Service early in 1971, after passage of the Organized Crime Control Act the previous year. Now courtroom sketches and news photos of these hooded figures, many of whom are former criminals themselves, are familiar to the public from such high-profile trials as the "Pizza Connection" case of 1987 in the Southern District of New York. There 18 men were convicted of operating an international heroin and cocaine ring that distributed more than $1.6 billion in drugs through pizza parlors in the Northeast and Midwest. The involvement of organized-crime "families" made this one of the many high-threat, multidefendant trials that required extensive security precautions. But Witness Security extends far beyond the courtroom. It involves creating new identities for witnesses and their dependents.

CARL VON REIN
USMS

ROXANNA LINDSTROM
USMS

TOP LEFT: *Detective Enforcement Officer Shaun Meakins checks prisoner security aboard a National Prisoner Transportation System flight.*

ABOVE: *A hooded member of the Witness Security Program is escorted into court to give testimony.*

LEFT: *Communications skills and equipment are vital to today's Marshals Service.*

Since 1971 more than 5,000 witnesses have entered the Witness Security Program. They and their family members are moved to another city under new identities and are provided all the services they need to help them become acclimated to the new community and to become self-sustaining as soon as possible. Witnesses enter the program on the recommendation of a U.S. attorney and the Criminal Division of the Department of Justice. Then the Marshals Service provides around-the-clock protection to such witnesses while they are in a threat environment and whenever they return to a danger area for pretrial conferences, trials, or other proceedings.

ABOVE: *Communications Specialist Benjamin Secundy monitors security for the District of Columbia courthouse.*

In 1987 the Witness Security (WITSEC) Program opened its Safesite and Orientation Center in Washington, D.C. The center provides a secure environment in which to interview and initiate witnesses and their families into the program. Closed-circuit television networks, intruder alarms, and sophisticated radio and telephone systems contribute to the security of the facility.

That same year, deputy marshals arrested Alphonse (Allie Boy) Carmine Persico, a reputed member of the Colombo organized crime family, who had been a fugitive for seven years. Deputies tracked him to an apartment in Hartford, Connecticut, where he was arrested for jumping a $250,000 bond. Persico had a criminal history of murder, fraud, extortion, assault, and loan sharking. Specialists at U.S. Marshals Service headquarters had constructed three lifesize busts of Persico as he would look seven years after he became a fugitive, and photos of these busts assisted deputies in conducting the interviews that led to his arrest.

Other Marshals Service fugitive investigations have involved escaped federal prisoners, probation and parole violators, and

ABOVE: *Fugitive Alphonse Persico is escorted from the Hartford, Connecticut, Federal Building. His arrest in November 1987 ended a seven-year manhunt by U.S. marshals.*

fugitives resulting from investigations by the Drug Enforcement Administration. In fact, deputy marshals arrest more fugitives under warrant each year than all other federal law-enforcement agencies combined. As of 1991 the Marshals Service was receiving approximately 78,000 federal warrants each year, more than 50 percent of which were felony warrants.

Some of the fugitive investigations have had their lighter side, as in the case of Samantha Lopez, who escaped from the Pleasonton (California) Correctional Institution while serving time for bank robbery. She also faced charges on murder and kidnapping. On November 6, 1986, her boy friend, Ronald McIntosh, landed a hijacked helicopter in the prison's recreation yard and flew away with her. The media had a field day with the "love birds" story, while deputy marshals tracked the pair to a shopping mall where they were arrested 10 days later as they were in the process of picking up their wedding rings.

In a famous 1985 case, the Marshals Service sent spurious invitations to a "free brunch" at the D.C. Convention Center to the last known address of a number of men and women wanted for

ABOVE: *Gamely disguised as the San Diego Chicken, a marshal helps round up fugitives at a "free brunch" staged by the Fugitive Investigative Strike Team (FIST).*

various criminal offenses. The invitations, from a fictitious sports television firm, offered free tickets to a Washington Redskins home football game and chances for a trip to the Super Bowl. As the fugitives arrived, they were greeted by deputy marshals costumed as ushers, cleaning personnel, caterers – even as the popular San Diego Chicken, a Big Bird-like character in a feathered outfit who appeared at football games. The fugitives were photographed frolicking around the big chicken (who had a gun strapped under his wing) before they were arrested. This operation was part of the ongoing Fugitive Investigative Strike Team (FIST), which the Marshals Service began in 1981.

Another successful FIST ruse occurred in 1986, when Deputy Joseph Bruer, Jr., posed as a mailman delivering a package to the last known address of a fugitive. Nicknamed "Mr. Zip," Bruer got the wanted man to the door to sign for a "special package," and his colleagues then made the arrest. The fugitive was at once delivered to the county jail.

In August 1981 a 19-month international hunt ended in the arrest of Christopher John Boyce in Port Angeles, Washington. Nicknamed "the Falcon," Boyce had escaped from the federal prison in Lopez, California, after he was convicted of selling U.S. secrets to the Soviets and sentenced to 40 years. Boyce was the first major fugitive arrested by the marshals after their responsibilities were expanded to include escapees from federal prison facilities. The following year, international terrorist Edwin P. Wilson was lured out of hiding in Libya and arrested by the Marshals Service after a two-year search. Wilson had close ties with terrorist groups and was wanted on charges of conspiracy to commit murder, transporting explosives, exporting defense articles, and acting as an agent of the Libyan government.

ABOVE: *Charged with violating U.S. Immigration Codes, the Bhagwan Shree Rajneesh is led away from the federal courthouse in Charlotte, North Carolina, in 1985.*

RIGHT: *Marshals escort former CIA agent Edwin Wilson from the courthouse in Alexandria, Virginia, after his 1982 conviction for smuggling guns to Libyan terrorists. Wilson was sentenced to a 15-year prison term and fined $200,000.*

In April 1988, Honduran millionaire Juan Matta-Ballesteros was arrested by deputy marshals at New York's John F. Kennedy Airport after his expulsion from the Dominican Republic in a well-planned operation. Allegedly one of the world's most notorious cocaine traffickers, Matta-Ballesteros was charged with drug trafficking and escape from custody.

The Marshals Service is also responsible for the management and disposal of seized and forfeited properties and assets, and, as of this writing, the service is managing more than $1.4 billion-worth of property seized from criminals. The program provides for central and efficient management and prompt disposal of assets seized by all Department of Justice agencies. A headquarters staff and eight field offices work to maximize the net return from seized property and reinvest the property and proceeds for law enforcement use.

The marshals have continued to work closely with the Bureau of Prisons. During the two-week uprising of Cuban prisoners at the Atlanta, Georgia, and Oakdale, Louisiana, federal penitentiaries in 1987, deputy marshals of the Special Operations Group assisted the Bureau of Prisons until a settlement was negotiated. The Cuban inmates were protesting the State Department's plan to return them to Fidel Castro's Cuba. During the uprising they ejected other prisoners from the facility, including four-time convicted murderer Thomas Silverstein, who was taken into custody by the marshals.

LEFT: *An industrial building inside the federal penitentiary at Atlanta smolders during the Cuban refugee uprising of November 24, 1987.*

BELOW: *A marshal searches and handcuffs a suspect as his partner covers him.*

In 1984 a new law made it a crime to hold American citizens hostage outside the United States. The first conviction under this statute was that of international terrorist Fawaz Younis, who was tried for air piracy in the 1985 hijacking in Lebanon of an airliner with two Americans aboard. Security for the 1989 trial of Younis, an accused member of Beirut's Amal militia, was extremely tight, and the faces of deputy marshals who escorted him during his trial were obliterated in publicity photos to ensure their safety.

The marshals' task of protecting the courts and the judiciary has become ever more demanding over time. During 1990 there were 496 reported threats against the federal judiciary — an almost 600 percent increase since 1980, when 48 threats were received. In December 1989, Federal Judge Robert Vance, of the Eleventh Circuit Court, was assassinated by a pipe bomb at his home in Birmingham, Alabama. The bomb had arrived in a package with the

return address of a judicial colleague to allay suspicion. Only two other federal judges had been killed for their official acts in the previous 200 years. U.S. Marshal Tom Greene of the Northern District of Alabama was on the scene within 45 minutes to begin a wide-reaching protective operation that began with Judge Vance's wife, who had been seriously injured in the explosion and taken to the hospital for surgery, and quickly encompassed all 19 judges of the Eleventh Circuit. Within 72 hours, three more mail bombs arrived, two at federal facilities in Atlanta and Savannah, the other at NAACP headquarters in Jacksonville, Florida. The bombs sent to Atlanta and Jacksonville were discovered and defused in time, but the third exploded, killing Robert E. Robinson, a civil rights attorney. For the next eight months, the Marshals Service protected all of the Eleventh Circuit judges 24 hours a day, at a cost of almost a quarter of a million dollars.

In 1983 the Marshals Service cooperated with federal agencies to implement the Court Security Officer (CSO) program as a vital element in the protection of the judicial process and court personnel. Under this program, CSOs are hired by contract to perform the building perimeter security functions; to screen people coming into the court buildings, and to augment the security

ABOVE: *Accused of espionage, prisoner Huseyin Yildirim leaves the federal court in Tampa, Florida, in 1988.*

TOP RIGHT: *Deputy Marshal Lydia Blakey provides security at the high-threat trial of accused Columbian drug lord Carlos Lehder Rivas in February 1987.*

RIGHT: *U.S. Justice Department photo of Lehder Rivas, who was convicted of smuggling tons of cocaine into Florida.*

needed for sensitive trials. Each year, these officers discover and intercept more and more weapons at federal courthouses. In 1990 the Court Security Officers prevented more than 137,000 weapons from being carried into courthouses and assisted in 97 arrests.

Deputy Marshal Lydia Blakely and hundreds of her colleagues provided extensive security arrangements for the 1987 trial of Carlos Lehder Rivas in Miami, Florida. Rivas was charged with importing tons of cocaine through northeast Florida and was considered one of the world's most powerful drug smugglers. Security for his trial cost the Marshals Service $2 million, but Rivas was convicted and sentenced to the maximum possible term – life without parole plus 135 years.

The marshals' resources were stretched thin again during the 1989 United Mine Workers of America strike, which spread from southwest Virginia to West Virginia and other Blue Ridge states. Eventually, more than 30,000 striking miners were involved, with frequent conflict between UMW members and those who wanted to cross picket lines to work. Deputy marshals from many districts worked with state and local police to maintain order, ensure access to coal fields and public utilities, and prevent violence among the factions involved.

LEFT: *A marshal patrols on St. Croix, Virgin Islands, in the wake of Hurricane Hugo, September 1989.*

RIGHT: *Ousted Panamanian dictator Manuel Noriega, taken into custody in Miami in January 1990 on charges of drug trafficking.*

BELOW: *A member of the American Indian Movement (AIM) is flanked by marshals on road-block duty at the Pine Ridge Reservation during the AIM takeover of Wounded Knee, South Dakota: March 1973.*

Natural disaster made demands on the Marshals Service in September 1989, when Hurricane Hugo struck the Virgin Islands. Some 200 prisoners escaped from jails during the devastating storm, and looting was rampant. Attorney General Richard Thornburgh sent the marshals to St. Croix and adjacent islands to work with local and military police and the FBI in restoring order.

In January 1990, the marshals took deposed Panamanian leader Manuel Noriega into custody in Miami on charges of drug trafficking. It was the culmination of an intensive joint effort with the DEA, the FBI, and U.S. Army Special Forces in Panama in what President George Bush had dubbed "Operation Just Cause."

The invasion of Panama had widespread U.S. public support, but the marshals have never flinched from carrying out their mandate in controversial cases as well, from the days of the fugitive slave laws to the 1973 suppression of the American Indian Movement (AIM) in its takeover of Wounded Knee, South Dakota. AIM forces were in occupation for 71 days before their May 8 surrender to U.S.

marshals, making Wounded Knee the second-longest civil disorder in American history, the longest being the Civil War.

Shorter in duration, but much larger in scope, was the marshals' involvement in the huge riots that convulsed Los Angeles in the spring of 1992. The trouble began when, at the end of April, an all-white California jury declined to convict several Los Angeles policemen who had been charged with the unprovoked beating of a black motorist named Rodney King. (The issue was not whether the beating had occurred – it had been videotaped by a bystander – but whether it could be justified.) Most Americans found the jury's decision shocking and distasteful, but in the black ghettos and Latin-American barrios of Los Angeles it was seen as something much worse: an intolerable provocation and a confirmation of long-held doubts about the fundamental equity of the U.S. system of justice. Violence erupted almost immediately and swelled to massive proportions in the next few days. Before the rioting ended, 58 people had been killed, nearly a billion dollars-worth of property damage had been done, and some 17,000 arrests had been made: as

so often happens in such cases, by far the greatest havoc had been wreaked in the very communities where the protest originated. In addition to local police and national guard units, some 1,200 federal law officers had been needed to help restore order, and of the latter, nearly one quarter had been U.S. marshals. It had been the largest single deployment of marshals in the twentieth century.

In 1989 the U.S. marshals celebrated their 200th year of law enforcement in American history, 200 years of performing a wide array of demanding and dangerous tasks. In K. Michael Moore they gained a new director – the first to be selected through the presidential appointment process. In the districts, as the service entered its third century, 20-year employees were retiring, creating opportunities for younger people attuned to the new ways of doing things. Professionalism, sound training, and commitment to duty marked this new generation of officers, and it was clear that the already high standards set by the Marshals Service would soon rise even higher.

TOP: *Marshals proudly display their merit citations.*

ABOVE: *The Bicentennial-issue marshal's badge.*

RIGHT: *On March 3, 1992, Henry Hudson succeeded K. Michael Moore as the new director of the 203-year-old Marshals Service.*

LEFT: *Rioting in the streets of Los Angeles in the aftermath of the Rodney King trial verdict: April 29, 1992.*

WANTED
BY U.S. MARSHALS

NOTICE TO ARRESTING AGENCY: Before arrest, validate warrant through National Crime Information Center (NCIC).

United States Marshals Service NCIC entry number: (NIC/_____).

NAME: WORTH, Stephen King

ALIAS: PINE, Patrick Nelson; BARTLEY, Patrick; PINE, Patrick; "HIPPY STEVE"; FREEMAN, Steve

DESCRIPTION:

Sex: .... MALE
Race: .... WHITE
Place of Birth: .... WASHINGTON, DC
Date(s) of Birth: .... DECEMBER 17, 1949
Height: .... 5'11"
Weight: .... 150 LBS.
Eyes: .... BROWN
Hair: .... BROWN
Skintone: .... MEDIUM
Scars, Marks, Tattoos: .... NONE
Social Security Number: 231-70-6216
NCIC Fingerprint Classification: .. NONE

SHOULD BE CONSIDERED ARMED AND DANGEROUS

WORTH was involved in a major drug trafficking organization that used UZI and MAC-11 sub-machine guns equipped with silencers.

WANTED FOR: DISTRIBUTION OF MARIJUANA

Warrant Issued: Eastern District of Virginia (Alexandria)
Warrant Number: 85-00010-A

DATE WARRANT ISSUED: January 14, 1985

MISCELLANEOUS INFORMATION: WORTH was part of a marijuana smuggling organiz that distributed nearly 300 tons of high-grade marijuana throughout the United States.

If arrested or whereabouts known, notify the local United States Marshals Office, (Telephone: _____).

If no answer, call United States Marshals Service Communications Center in McLean, Virginia.
Telephone (800)336-0102: (24 hour telephone contact) NLETS access code is VAUSMOOOO.
(800)423-0719 (TDD)
PRIOR EDITIONS ARE OBSOLETE AND NOT TO BE USED

Form
(R

INDEX

(Numerals in italics indicate illustrations)